GLIMMER of HOPE

Book Two

Rick Lasley

outskirts press

Glimmer of Hope
Book 2
All Rights Reserved.
Copyright © 2022 Rick Lasley
v2.0

The opinions expressed in this manuscript are solely the opinions of the author and do not represent the opinions or thoughts of the publisher. The author has represented and warranted full ownership and/or legal right to publish all the materials in this book.

This book may not be reproduced, transmitted, or stored in whole or in part by any means, including graphic, electronic, or mechanical without the express written consent of the publisher except in the case of brief quotations embodied in critical articles and reviews.

Outskirts Press, Inc.
http://www.outskirtspress.com

ISBN: 978-1-9772-5670-6

Cover Photo © 2022 Greg Tate. All rights reserved - used with permission.

Outskirts Press and the "OP" logo are trademarks belonging to Outskirts Press, Inc.

PRINTED IN THE UNITED STATES OF AMERICA

*To my daughter, Ms. Lauren Lasley, and all pre-educators like her, who,
despite the conditions that exist in education today,
answered the call to be a teacher and
transform the lives of children – forever changing humanity.*

Preface

As long as there is love, kindness, AND the existence of pre-teachers entering the pipeline, despite these conditions we are working in, a glimmer of hope for education always exists....

If you read Book 1, *Humanity in Peril*, it likely did a number on your psyche (unless you are a public educator). If any public educator was surprised by the details shared in my first book, I may have missed my mark and the conditions in education that I described are very isolated. I venture to say this is not the case, and countless educators across the nation are nodding their heads in agreement for what they may have read in Book 1, *Humanity in Peril*.

The hate, negativity, and lack of respect this world has far too much of these days (as mentioned in Book 1) needs to stop. Individuals and communities need to consider what is most important for society and humanity moving forward in order to get back to some form of positive ground whereby people (as well as elected officials) respect the opinions of others without hostility. Our nation's children have been sitting back taking notes these past few years. As singer, songwriter, and producer Quincy Jones so aptly wrote in his lyrics so many years ago that still ring true today - "War is not the answer, for only love can conquer hate" ... I feel strongly these words had as little to do with the act of war as it did with the clashes between people who see the world differently. Our nation must find a way to come to peace within our own boundaries, or this country will certainly perish....

My wife, Angela, and I have four children. As I mentioned before this publication, we are very proud of all of them. For the reasons that I have now published a second book, I am especially proud of our daughter, Lauren. As of the completion of this manuscript and pre-publication, Lauren has successfully completed her student teaching experience and has graduated from the University of Kentucky with a BA in Music Education and minor in Math. She has taken the Praxis exams for both music and HS mathematics and has passed both. I advised Lauren to take the Praxis for math just in case she needed to pursue a math teaching position until she could find a music position. The level of competition for open positions is much higher for music than it is in math. For math, in some areas of the state we live in, there are simply no applicants!

Unlike the focus of Book 1, *Humanity in Peril*, the focus of this book is on the "glimmers of hope," like Lauren, who exist to keep the future of education moving in a positive direction. While very similar concerns and events are featured in these journal entries (based on the 2022 spring semester at Apollo High School) as those in Book 1 (based on the 2021 fall semester), the theme yields a much more HOPEFUL message for the people and events that support and positively impact teachers and students.

My hope is that by reading both books, communities and our elected officials will turn **MUCH NEEDED** attention **BACK** to education.

Unless proper funding is adequately budgeted to school districts to increase teacher salaries and support staff wages, ***unless*** the proper resources are allocated to schools in order to support a **trained** staff to provide students the mental health/emotional health they desperately need, ***unless*** communities and parents find positive ways to support their schools as well as teachers and bring the **RESPECT** and **APPEAL** back to education in general, my efforts and reasons **FOR** publishing these books will have been in vain.

As of the publishing of *Glimmer of Hope*, I am now a retired educator of thirty-two years. If I had followed through with my first desire after graduating high school, I would have at least gone in the direction of architecture. Who knows if I would have been accepted to even start, but that was my purpose for selecting the university I attended. Initially, I had ZERO thoughts on making a career out of education. Fortunately for me and my mounting college debt, my passion for working in a more service-oriented career became clear to me by the end of my first year in college. My connection to education became even more solidified at the point that I watched the movie **Dead Poets Society** (1988), starring Robin Williams as "Mr. Keating". Making an impact on the lives of young adults as they solidified their own purpose and passion in life would serve me much better than ***anything*** I could have chosen to do.

Although I would not have been happy, I certainly could have made a much better life for myself and my family had I followed through with my initial desire to pursue architecture. I have worked alongside countless other educators who either <u>**were**</u> engineers, scientists, or other "higher-ranked" careers and chose to become teachers, OR they easily <u>**could**</u> have pursued those interests. Like me, these individuals followed their passion and their desire to impact and change the lives of young adults to help prepare them for their future. Those of us who ***truly*** have a passion for teaching LOVE what we do and have made th decision to continue our careers as educators, regardless of the pay or the conditions. The concern that I have is that there are far fewer passionate educators working today than what existed thirty-two years ago. ***Doesn't it make sense that our nation needs to work to find more?***

I would like to thank ALL the passionate and dynamic educators I have worked alongside in my thirty-two year career. As I have mentioned in Book 1, I strongly feel that each one of us carries a small amount of those we have been in the trenches with over the years. I am truly blessed for the connections I have made and the tremendous individuals I am fortunate to have called my peers. I wish you all the very best as you continue to make an impact on the future of humanity...

I would especially like to thank Misty Dilback, who is one of a handful of extraordinary educators with whom I have had the pleasure of working with over my career. Mrs. Dilback is one of the "Rock Star" teachers who is highlighted in this book for her ability to make learning real and for knowing the incredible difference making connections and forming relationships with her students can make. As if that were not enough, she was instrumental in helping with a vast majority of the editing that made this book a possibility. If there are any remaining edits that were missed, it is most likely that ***my stubbornness*** got in my way of making the change! Thank you, Mrs. Dilback, for your support in the process to get Book 2 published. I look forward to seeing your continued impact on your students and education in general... **BEYOND 30 years!**

Author's Note

Other than my wife and children, the names of any individuals mentioned in this book have been changed to protect their identity. Most names have been withheld for the same reason.

January 4, 2022 ("One Day Closer…") - So, by the grace of a construction "miracle" and several DCPS (Daviess County Public Schools) adults putting in _**days**_ over Christmas Break to make it happen (including Apollo's "Rock Star" Head Custodian), we were able to slide into the start of this semester in our new addition on two wheels. As the teachers had a professional development day yesterday to prepare for the start of this semester (and, YES, make final preparations in NEW classrooms), we worked around painters, locker installers, electricians, and maintenance personnel. On this first day of school to start the Spring Semester, we could still smell the paint drying….

Truth be told, this new addition to Apollo HS is an absolute blessing and something very much needed as we have been working in a dilapidated building with inadequate space for 21st Century Teaching, not to mention the fire alarm system, HVAC system and any system you can imagine being outdated and near unserviceable.

With the new addition, we have a state-of-the-art engineering facility on one end of the building to support a growing Engineering Program (and a team of engineering teachers that compares to NONE anywhere in the state of Kentucky!). On the other end of the building, we have an agriculture facility to support our state-recognized Ag and FFA Program equipped with the latest tools and resources enabling us to offer Horticulture, Small Animal, and Ag Construction systems. In between these two dynamic academies, we have twenty-seven regular classrooms filled with our Math Department and Social Studies Department (with a few Special Ed. Teachers).

The "curse" that comes along with the move into this brand new facility is that the decades-old bus drop-off and parent drop-off procedures have traded sides of our growing building footprint, AND it is only mid-year, which creates logistical nightmares for staff, parents and students.

Changes in procedures are inevitable to start most school years and are far more tolerable for parents and even teachers to stomach. With the way the Fall Semester ends coupled with Christmas Break, it leaves very few opportunities to communicate.

The Leadership Team did our best to prepare our parents for the NEW morning drop-off routine. If it weren't for the help of several of our DCPS Maintenance Staff standing in entrance ways with signs saying, "Do Not Enter," "Students Only," or "Exit Only," parent drop-off for this first day of a new semester would have been utter chaos. It was because of a miscommunication that matters became a little worse than what they could have been when an adult was blocking off one of the exit points available for our parents, but that was quickly remedied. Still, with adults available to "force" parents into the "funnel" we had provided and a system recommended by civil engineers/architects when the construction project was first envisioned, we had parents backed up completely around our campus.

As I approached one of our maintenance department helpers to get him straight on the process for parents exiting, I asked him to relay the plan (for TWO drop points and exits) to each of the parents who pull up with their child. The FIRST parent to roll down her window to allow communication responded with, "All of you should be shot and fired!"

THIS is the state in which we find ourselves working through what is now a **_second_** year of pandemic conditions. Parents who have ZERO patience for us to work through the FIRST day of a brand-new procedure (after it was communicated twice over the past ten days with map included) and parents who have ZERO support for our decision-making (that is ALWAYS based on best-practice and student-safety in mind). I have mentioned before that we **_absolutely_** have parents who support everything we are doing. We just do not hear from them daily or even weekly, as much as we are trashed on social media or berated directly by the growing number of adults who question our **_every_** move....

Sensing that the leadership team needed to regroup and discuss any issues we saw at the parent drop-off procedure this morning, I sent a quick invite for the administrators and school law enforcement personnel to meet at 9:15 am. At the meeting, I quickly determined that the team was split on what should be done to alleviate this traffic flow pattern for parent drop-offs. A couple on the team felt that the circling of the campus by our parents should be avoided altogether. With construction (renovation of **_existing_** building) still going on that is blocking a couple of campus entry points, we HAD to give the civil engineering-designed plan the benefit of our efforts (despite what anyone felt about it). After showing the Leadership Team the original plan outlining the new parent drop-off route that was drawn up by the civil engineers over three years ago (September 2018 to be exact), I felt that the team understood a little better the magnitude of what we were dealing with… and that **_for now_**, it was out of our hands and up to us to make it work.

Because this was our first day with students, it was also our first opportunity since the end of last semester to explain to them how the dismissal procedures (with the line-up of parents nearby) would affect them. Although we have never used our Eagles Nest Live (ENL) broadcast in the afternoon for something of this magnitude, I felt that the visual aid in **_showing_** the students on a map what they should do to prepare for parents to pick them up or for student drivers to leave and avoid a traffic jam was worth the effort.

I also wanted to send out another communication to our parents prior to dismissal to explain the TWO exit points and our suggestions to avoid heavy traffic. We set this up and also prepared for more adults to be present to help our students in the student parking lot exit, according to the plan that was explained to them on ENL, and also help our parents keep the traffic flowing.

The summation of the day after all our efforts to smooth out the first day of afternoon pick-up procedures... a grand total of twenty minutes for our campus to be emptied from the time that our dismissal bell sounded at 3:15 pm. I would venture to say this is considered GOOD for a first-run of a new procedure that can only improve! What was disheartening to hear was our front entrance teacher on duty coming into the office to drop off her radio exclaim, "Boy, our parents are SO mad...!"

While I was completely consumed and distracted all day with our new routine and our parents' disappointing reaction to Day 1, I found out that two students were busted this morning for "smoking" in one of the brand-new restrooms and at the end of the day found out that we have a total of fifteen individuals quarantined from recent virus exposure or positive tests (two staff and thirteen students). Before Christmas Break, we were averaging less than two quarantines per day!

These pandemic conditions, our lack of parental support (more like **_blind criticism_**), and our student apathy/continued lack of engagement create a "perfect storm" that is consuming the S.S. Education. As I arrived home, my wife Angela could read the expression on my face. All I had to say was, "One day closer to retirement...."

January 5, 2022 (Day 2) - If you can believe it (based on my explanation of Day 1), the second day of the semester started out much better. By initiating the two exit points and drop offs from beginning to end, the traffic kept flowing and did not back up hardly at all. What made this better is the fact that the parent line was completely removed from the streets and not holding up the bus traffic. Our second day of a **_brand-new_** procedure, and it seems to be running smoothly?! I realize that things can change once the maintenance personnel exit their temporary posts, leaving parents to freely enter where they will, but my thoughts are more concerned with the fact that society has reached the point that it has **no** patience, **no** respect, and **no** compassion.

There was very little time for these thoughts to consume me as this day started. On the morning ENL broadcast, one of the assistant principals explained to the students a few things to consider as they enter the new building, especially after realizing that students were all trying to use the main stairwell (down and up) when classes changed and that nobody was using the stairwells at the ends. I also took the opportunity to speak to our students about what process DCPS will use to determine a traditional snow day vs. virtual instruction day in the case of inclement weather. Tomorrow, we are forecasted to get snow that will likely cause school to be canceled.

While on ENL with everyone's attention in the building (ok, **most**), I took the opportunity to speak to the students about the importance of being respectful and being patient while working through new systems and processes. This is one of those moments that I take a quick step up on the proverbial "soapbox" and coach our students on being a part of the GOOD in the world... I'm not always sure it registers enough to make a difference, but it is well worth the effort.

Being that we were expecting snow and potentially a traditional snow day, we had communication to prepare for our parents to let them know our process for snow day vs. virtual instruction. Today was also an important day in that all first semester grades were due to be posted by 3:00 pm. I also had an idea to make some signs and add cones providing two lanes to help aid in the process for parent pick-up. If that weren't enough, I was surprised by a TV news reporter showing up and wanting to take some footage of the new building and classrooms.

On the bright side of things, our cafeteria staff has not needed me to help run my provisional cashier stand at lunch. Of the eighty-plus school days in the fall semester, I feel certain that I was needed on seventy or more days because our staff was missing four or more of its sixteen members. On those days, our athletic director and I filled in as cashier to help at two of our five food lines, leaving the ladies **only** covering for two **more** positions. It is a relief to me knowing that these ladies have not needed my help because there is <u>**no way**</u> I could have made the time to be there the ninety minutes it takes to get through three lunch shifts.

Because I was still waiting on the signage I needed to place onto cones for the parent pick-up procedure, I spent a little time this afternoon walking the building and stopping by a couple of classrooms in the new addition. There was one teacher who had started a brand-new teaching routine that I wanted to see, and I wanted to see what the transition between classes looked like in the new building and between the new and original building. The transition is still a little jammed with a vast-majority of our students using the main stairwell, but the better part of my trip around the school was spent mingling and connecting with students, as well as getting the "thumbs up" from the teacher with the new routine.

At dismissal today, despite a handful of parents who drove in the wrong direction a couple of times to completely avoid the line and take advantage of a fast pick-up and quick getaway, the pick-up and departure process went much smoother. Adding an exit lane and designating Left Turn and Right Turn ONLY lanes sped up the process and enabled us to empty our campus in fifteen minutes! Day 2 of a <u>**brand-new**</u> process...

On my way home, I feel much better today than I did yesterday. Again, if ONLY people had patience and supported us in doing our jobs! The dagger that I didn't need on my way home was finding out that something happened with several of our teachers and the posting of semester-ending grades. On our first snow day of the school year, we will have some cleaning up to do so that we can post grades to transcripts and help our seniors get what they need to apply for college.

January 7, 2022 - Yesterday's weather created a traditional Snow Day that would be made up later in the year. I had started down the road to come to school around 8:30 am expecting a very light snow only to get to Apollo HS where two-plus inches had already accumulated. Because the snow was not scheduled to stop until afternoon, I left the vehicle running and went inside the school to send a couple of emails and also send our head custodian home. He lives a distance away from school and has several backroads to travel.

Because the area between Daviess and Hancock counties received around four inches of snow and especially due to the single digit temperatures overnight, DCPS announced that today would be our first Virtual Instruction Day where students are to log in to a Google Meet set up by their teacher and have a minimum of thirty minutes of instruction or review. Because the roads are in such poor condition, the challenge is for some adults who do not have good enough internet service to make it into their classrooms and follow through with the expectations. Regarding students, a portion of our families do not have internet at all, or their service is not good enough to sustain a connection in order to fully participate. Regardless of connectivity, virtual instruction is not at all ideal (we ALL learned this the hard way last year!). For that reason, we can only hope for a very limited number of virtual instruction days between now and the end of the year.

While the teachers were teaching, I made sure the Leadership Team and I carried out our weekly meeting because we had some very important topics to cover. While the majority of the team was present, I also gave the option for any who wanted to attend virtually.

Among the topics we covered, the three that prompted the most discussion were our new parent pick-up and drop-off procedures, the deadline and evidence we still needed to collect for our accreditation review visit, and grades/failure reports that we needed to look through once the mid-year grades were finally posted (waiting on three teachers as of this morning). For the new pick-up and drop-off procedures, we decided that the most recent upgrades to the process were good enough to sustain the procedure. However, at the point that the adults are no longer present for the morning and afternoon routines, there would be too many individuals (students AND parents) choosing to circumvent the entire setup. For this reason, we agreed the addition of a gate or two was necessary (to be closed ONLY for the morning and afternoon routines so that nobody can try to enter an "exit ONLY" location). We also wanted to go so far as to ask DCPS maintenance for an additional entrance/exit into the student parking lot. After two days of our new routine, we have discovered that unless an additional exit is made available, our parents coming onto campus to pick up students, along with our students who drive and are leaving campus, will always be crossing traffic and using the same entrance/ exit. This is not a good set-up and will make for some volatile interactions in the future.

With this in mind, I sent a plea to the architects, our DCPS maintenance supervisor, and our superintendent that included a rationale and maps showing the current and requested needs to make the set-up much better. I expect that on Monday I will be having a conversation with our DCPS maintenance supervisor to go over what can be done in the short term and what (if anything) can be done in the long term to help with our AM and PM procedures. Until then, administrators and dismissal staff need to work to maintain what we had established after our Day 1 improvements and shoot for an afternoon emptying within a fifteen-minute timeframe.

Days like this can be very productive due to the fact that you are interacting with very few individuals, so for my last duty before leaving, I worked with my secretary to send the weekly newsletter that includes a calendar of events out to our parents (and staff). In this letter that I create each week, I take some time to ask our parents to **"give us a break and, once again, PLEASE BE PATIENT..."** in the most professional words I could put together. To make sure that I was not coming across as too bitter, I asked my secretary to send it first to our lead guidance counselor and one of our "Dynamo" instructional coaches to get their advice. The end result was the approval from both to send as-is....

I am ready to rest and recharge this weekend after three shortened days of work this week!

January 11, 2022 - These past two days have been a stark reminder that we continue to grind through a pandemic, and it is something we had better try to address. We are, much like this point last year, scrambling to cover all the adults who are unable to be here in the building due to positive tests or quarantines. In two days, we have had eight adults TEST positive and the need for thirty-eight students to be quarantined (positive themselves or in contact with a positive). Since the return from Christmas Break, I have not been given any official attendance reports for Apollo HS, but I know that our attendance cannot be above ninety percent yesterday or today. I will be finding this out soon....

Because we are working through more adults being out, today was my first day this semester to be called to help as a cashier at lunch. I had stopped by yesterday just to see how they were doing and ended up helping during the 3rd lunch shift. The request for me to help today is one I readily accepted because I needed to get out of the managerial work I have been doing in the office (parent drop-off procedures, filling in for teachers, etc.). Making direct connections with the students is the one thing that I can always come back to that always brightens my day.

I had a visit from one of our district leaders today, whom I informed about being very close to reaching a point where it would be hard for us to function as a school because of the missing adults. Sadly, it does not appear that it will be letting up any time soon based on the cases that are being reported in the Owensboro community. Although DCPS will continue down the path of an "in-person learning or bust" model, I informed him to prepare that "bust" may happen soon.

To clarify my viewpoint on in-person learning, I COMPLETELY AGREE that we need to avoid virtual learning at ALL costs and that it was one of the worst things we could have done to our students LAST year (we will be working through the effects of the decisions we made and the 2021 school year for several years). And yet, a fine line still exists between just how much your staff can take and load onto its shoulders in times like this AND all the while maintain effective teaching/learning. Some very lasting effects need continued consideration, while at the same time trying to salvage in-person learning....

Teachers are covering for each other during their planning periods. The fact that they are finally being given this option for a slight increase in their pay (planning is supposed to already be factored into their daily wage) is irrelevant for the argument I am making. Working them harder during the day without the option to plan, put grades in, make copies, etc. just means that they are going to take more of their own time (and their family's time) to get it done. This will increase their stress and create more opportunities for them to be sick and absent (whether sick or just needing to "take a day to breathe"). As I have mentioned before, the current state that educators are working through as a result of this pandemic (apathy and absenteeism in our students, social-emotional and mental health of our students, lost learning, etc.) has given plenty of very strong (aka, "Rock Star") teachers the thought of retiring at the first point they are able. For many, this will mean retiring (whether they can afford it or not) after twenty-seven years of service. This act, coupled with the lack of candidates graduating from colleges/universities with certification to teach, will be **_catastrophic_** to education over the next couple of years.

Rather than going down the same path in this argument that I have several times previously (the journal I started back in August 2021), I will vent a little on the side that I firmly believe that we educators are partly contributing to this problem. Whether anyone wants to agree with this or not, an invisible wedge is being driven between educators over this past year. This wedge is making a distinct separation between those who are vaccinated and keep up the regimen of getting boosters when they are available and those who have either chosen to not get vaccinated at all OR those who were vaccinated and decline ever getting a booster shot (the effects of those initial vaccinations will NOT last forever!). By and large, those who have elected to continue the regimen of vaccination and boosters are the ones who are covering for the individuals that have elected not to. I fully understand that some individuals are advised or recommended NOT to get vaccinated by their doctor because of a current health condition, but too many educators still remain who elect not to get vaccinated because the virus was **_politicized_** from the very beginning nearly two years ago today! *[While I COMPLETELY agree that educators, health care workers, and other public servants are put in a VERY difficult position in times like this, my point is that we must find a way to REMOVE THE WEDGE and stay respectfully united in our mission and our work.]*

I firmly believe that our nation, especially, is still battling this original virus and the variants like the current omicron is because of MEDIA and the way that politicians today make EVERYTHING a partisan-battle where decisions are made based NOT on what is in the country's best interest, but INSTEAD what will make the other party "look bad". Media outlets are just as guilty in "taking sides" and reporting their viewpoints and opinions rather than sticking with facts and letting people inform their own decisions.

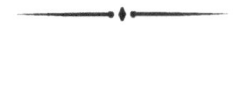

On a totally different subject and mindset that made me smile today, I walked into my office this morning to see that "Tommy" had delivered his bicycle on my promise at the end of last semester to get him some new tires. At the end of Book 1, you may recall that my last journal entry detailed a visit by "Tommy" riding his bicycle as I was getting into my truck to leave school. I can tell you that his mind has not stopped thinking about this since I spoke with him about it on my way out of the building on December 17, just before the start of Christmas Break. Since the semester had started, he has made a point to see me and talk to me about his bike and what he needed to do to help me fix it.

Yesterday, I told him that I needed to see what size tires to order so that we get the correct specs that his bike and rims needed. One of my assistant principals texted me this morning while I was on my way to school stating that "Tommy" was found waiting at the front doors at 6:40 am with his bike. Our front doors are not open and very few adults start to arrive before 7:00 am! The assistant principal had "Tommy" park his Schwinn Beach Cruiser bicycle right beside my desk so I wouldn't miss it....

After making the order for the tires and new tubes, I explained to "Tommy" that he may want to take it back home that afternoon because his new tires would not be delivered until Friday (knowing the weather may be suitable enough for him to put a few more miles on those tires the remainder of this week!). I told him to be sure to bring his bike back on Monday, and I would have our head agriculture teacher put the new tires on for him.

As I helped "Tommy" back his bike out of my office and into the hallway towards the front door, we continued to talk about the work that we were going to do on his bike (he is SO PROUD of this bike and would be devastated without it!). I continued watching him as he carefully made his way out the door and onto the sidewalk, weaving in and out of parked parent vehicles waiting for their students to arrive after dismissal. "Tommy" safely crossed Gemini Street, and I lost sight of him as he made his way home....

January 14, 2022 (running on fumes...) - This past week has been a tough one to manage as our adult positive cases and quarantines continue to climb. We had a total of sixteen certified teachers out of the building today with eight of them positive or quarantined due to contact. This meant that our certified staff members were at eighty-percent in attendance. Our classified staff were also just as affected by positive cases or quarantines, which left many of us administrators, instructional coaches, and guidance staff scrambling to help where we could. Teachers were giving up their planning time to help cover for their peers in an effort to maintain some semblance of teaching and learning. Based on what we have endured today and yesterday, I am hoping that we have reached the "benchmark" for what Apollo can safely manage as far as staffing goes, thereby leading to the decision to go virtual for a time period. Although there are no current plans of the like from the District Office, I have been telling people to "be prepared in the case that it happens."

Thinking far beyond Apollo HS and on a much larger scale for education in general... how much longer can we continue working in these conditions? What if two years from now, the same conditions exist because of the next variant and the faction of our nation who are hell-bent on remaining unvaccinated? Enough is enough, so I decided to send the following communication to the Apollo Staff:

> Apollo Staff - Please read the entire contents of this email. I will keep it as brief as possible, **but we need everyone at Apollo on the same page** as we continue to navigate through this pandemic:

- There will not be any announcements today regarding next week from the District Office. The plan for now is to monitor staff availability over the weekend and make the call on Monday. **Keeping this in mind, please be fair and responsible in considering the following**:
  » Today we have had a total of 16 certified, 9 classified individuals out. Of these 25, 11 have had a positive test at some point (some CAN return on Tuesday).
  » How many other positives do we have? <u>**We all need to agree (for everyone's health and safety) to get tested if you have the tell-tale symptoms.**</u>
  » <u>*Vaccinations/Boosters*</u> - This part may upset some people and go against personal beliefs, but it is not intended to. We are all reaching the 1-year anniversary when most of us received our 1st vaccination. For those who were vaccinated and have not yet received a Booster, you are considered "unvaccinated." I personally feel it is our duty to continue maintaining the vaccinations and boosters against the virus. The lack of vaccinations is what is allowing this virus to continue *at the level that it is*. Regardless if you agree with this last statement, I hope that you can agree and see (after two years now) that <u>we will continue to work through this pandemic</u> and adapt the best we can as educators for a longer period of time. *I also hope that we can all agree that these conditions <u>are not fun</u> and that these very conditions jeopardize the future of education*... Please consider taking up the vaccination/booster regimen. Bravo to those of you who have....
  » For this weekend and moving forward, please be sure to keep your administrator updated as to your status (whether you are sick, found to be positive, etc.) so that we can accurately monitor and inform the board office of our staff needs for Tuesday.

Even if we go virtual at some point in the near future, after school events will be allowed to continue, unless the team cannot function due to positives and/or quarantines.

Again, please understand the professional nature that is intended in this communication. Like every one of you, I am "sick" of working in these conditions. If we want the conditions to change, then I feel we all need to be the 'change-agents' to help make it happen...

I hope all of you have a restful and healthy three-day weekend.

There are a few who would feel that my communication was inappropriate. I am hoping that a vast majority feel otherwise. As principal of Apollo HS, better yet, as an educator who has devoted his life to this career, I cannot sit back and watch as the walls come crumbling down around us...

Because the leadership team would be pulling double and triple duty covering in multiple directions today, I made sure to keep our weekly leadership meeting as short as possible. Our main topic of discussion was what we should do to prepare our staff, and especially our teachers, for virtual instruction (if it needs to happen). Most of the team agreed that we should wait until we know how to answer questions that teachers will be asking to send out anything definitive as far as our expectations. We left the meeting hoping that the communication may come as soon as that afternoon. As you can see in my email communication that was sent at the very end of the day today, the district communication never happened.

The past two days, I have covered for one of our custodians during lunch (cleaning and taking out trash in an isolated eating area) due to our day custodial staff being reduced by thirty-three percent. Today, I spent the lunch period helping cashier at "my" Global Fare Line. It was therapeutic for me being among the students again, connecting with them and giving as many of them a hard time as I could. Most of the students react positively to my efforts, as can be witnessed in their smile or banter back. The students are what keep ALL of us educators going!

January 19, 2022 - Thanks to Martin Luther King Day, this past weekend was a welcome relief for us in education - not so much that we desperately needed a break only nine days into this semester, but we needed time to get healthy. For Apollo HS, thankfully, our number of staff members positive and/or quarantined is decreasing (by half or more), but the numbers in other schools in the district are doubling. Due to the fact that our district has had even more out these past two days than what we had Friday, we have been forced to provide virtual instruction (DCPS@home) for our students. Based on the way that these numbers have been going, it is not likely to change before this week ends. Once again, I hope I am wrong! Adding to an already tough decision-making status for the district personnel, the afternoon forecast is calling for a rain to ice to snow and the potential of three inches before it is done.

Yesterday and today have given the construction crews "free reign" on the building to continue their work, without worry of anyone getting in their way. This has already been the case for the Phase 4 contractors who have completely closed off the 100's section and have it freely to themselves to ransack and renovate. Let's see if this fact will allow them to complete this section based on the timeline that was originally advertised: 100's complete by the end of May 2022 and ready to move into the 300's section by the start of summer break. I would sure love to see ONE construction project that actually finishes on time!

On the other hand, the most disappointing aspect of the new building construction (completely different construction company than Phase 4) was that it was **_supposed to be 100% complete_** and ready for us to move in by August 1, 2021! What's even more disappointing is that this company had led us on up until late April, making us believe that it was going to happen!! As of TODAY (yes, Jan. 19, 2022), the building is still being painted, lights being hung, lockers being installed, no breakers connected to our welding booths, downspouts not fully complete, and the amphitheater in front of the building at 10% completion. Based on this and a list of "punch" items (a list of any work that still needs to be completed or **_corrected_**) that is incredibly long, I can see work on the new building being done through the end of March!

Deep breath… Move on to something else… Focus on the POSITIVE…!

The GOOD thing about days like today and yesterday is that we can carry on with meetings, even if they have to be virtual. Small meetings (ten to fifteen individuals) are completely safe to continue, especially when everyone can find space to distance. The Apollo HS SBDM (Site-Based Decision Making) Council followed these guidelines to continue plans for our regular meeting yesterday. It is more trouble to postpone the meeting and reschedule because of all the paperwork and communication that it involves. We were able to have our meeting and take care of the items needed yesterday without any issues. Not that heading up these meetings has been a troublesome experience for me in any capacity, I just realized that I have only four more SBDM meetings that I am responsible for as principal. The vast majority of my SBDM parent and teacher connections and the meetings themselves have been a positive experience over my twenty years as a principal. My plans are to inform these council members of my decision to retire in a closed session of the March meeting, just prior to letting the staff know. This will allow the council time to be trained for the search and hire of a new principal, along with an adequate posting period and the hiring of the next principal by the middle of June (at the latest). My request to the superintendent when I informed him in late November of my final decision to retire was to follow the timeline of being given the opportunity to remain principal of Apollo HS through the end of this year without the worry of anyone "looking past me" in my final days of my career in education. I am hoping this is not seen as selfish - I simply want to be able to work until my last day and not be seen as "in the way"....

Around 11:00 am today, having heard no direction from the district office regarding the weather or plans for tomorrow, I went ahead and sent out an email to all staff that the building would be closed at 3:00 pm today. I wanted to be sure that everyone was aware that the temperature would be dropping and that the rain may turn to ice before snow. There is no reason why we shouldn't play it safe and get everyone home, including our evening custodians.

On my way home today, leaving just before 3:00 pm myself due to my forty-minute drive home, the official message went out that DCPS would be going virtual for tomorrow and Friday due to the weather conditions coupled with our inability to function at full capacity due to staff outages. Virtual learning is the worst thing for kids right now (considering what they went through this past year!), but it is the best we can provide at the moment... Here's hoping that healthier days are ahead!

January 21, 2022 - Hopefully, today marked the last "DCPS@ Home" day needed for the remainder of this school year. This may be a long-shot – considering we have around ten more weeks of winter weather to get through and the omicron variant is still producing posi- tive cases among the community. As far as DCPS adults are concerned, the positive cases over this past week have greatly reduced, at least to the point that we will be in person and "try this again" on Monday.

This morning we had our weekly Leadership Team meeting a little later than usual, considering there were no students in the building, and some of our leadership team members were working from home. The biggest item on the agenda for today was to go over our failure report for each grade level. Before the meeting, I had taken the failure report spreadsheet that was generated by our guidance office secretary and manipulated it to illustrate the number of students in each grade who were failing and how many courses in each grade level were failed. I also made a comparison to the same failure data that was collected for Fall 2017 and Fall 2018 so that we could see how far off the current data is with respect to "normal times."

This data comparison revealed everything we expected to see: the number of students failing at least one class, the number of students failing multiple classes, AND the total number of courses failed overall had greatly increased compared to Fall 2018. In some cases, the numbers had nearly doubled. As I went through each tab on this spreadsheet and explained what the manipulation revealed and highlighted, I asked the leadership team to share their thoughts or share any trends that they may have noticed. More importantly, I asked them what we could do here at Apollo HS to help reduce the number of failures moving forward.

Our lead guidance counselor shared that with all we have tried this past semester (knowing our students are struggling more than ever), these numbers were **_depressing_**. In _his_ words, "These are **_our_** kids...." The most frustrating aspect of the data we were looking at is the number of students who had failed four, five, and even all six of their classes. I explained to the leadership team that the answer wouldn't be as easy as sending them all to the district alternative school. WE had to find some solution at Apollo and not wait for the district or the state department to tell us what needed to be done. I asked the leadership team to dig deep and think as far outside the box as possible to come up with solutions that we could implement to make our students more successful... the sooner the better!

A perfect example of one of the better outside the box ideas that we have come up with was the creating and hiring of our Student Success Coach. Although he is not normally a part of our leadership team meetings, I had asked him to join us this day (considering that several of the students listed on the failure report were on his "caseload"). As our conversation this morning continued, the SSC's caseload grew, and we also were given insights from him on connections he had made so far (his first official day of employment in this role was December 6th). He also shared the method of his approach with the students, some needing daily contact and some just needing weekly updates. Although there was not enough time after Dec. 6 to make any major impact on his caseload of students, I am certain that this SSC position will be a game-changer for several of the students on this failure report between now and the end of the year. IF ONLY we had the ability to hire for this position back in August!

One of the assistant principals reminded us that as an MTSS (Multi-Tiered Support System) effort, we are looking at adjusting our schedule so that there is a period each day that could be used for intervention or remediation. The only problem is this schedule would not come into effect until the start of the next school year. Still, what we are going through now will certainly help us not only explain the need for the remediation time, but it should also allow us to obtain buy-in from a vast majority of the staff. The bottom line is that we **HAVE TO** do something to fix the amount of students failing....

One other item mentioned by our lead guidance counselor was that many of the students on the multiple failure list had zero support from home and that many of them had little sense of self-worth. Our chances of making any positive difference with these students would be small unless these issues were first corrected. I told the team that this was a very valid point that needed consideration and that it would take time **_outside the classroom_** for us to make any difference in the social/emotional/mental health of our students. Although we discussed very little else in this meeting today, this one topic left the team plenty to be thinking about.

The rest of this day had me preparing multiple communications to go out to staff, lead teachers, and Apollo families via the weekly newsletter that goes out each Friday afternoon. I am ready (as we ALL are) to put this week behind us. Tomorrow, I have an opportunity to attend a college basketball game with my wife and one of our sons. I am looking forward to getting my mind off work and the quality family time that becomes more rare as each day passes....

January 25, 2022 - These past two days have been a blessing as we have returned to in-person instruction to start this week. After taking the time last week to "get well," Apollo staff has been pretty much full force. Today, we had one positive adult case and one adult who had to stay home with a sick child. Beyond that, EVERYONE was ready to come back to work. If you can believe it, we were also 100% staffed in the cafeteria for the ***first time in over a year***! Sixteen of sixteen cafeteria staff all reported today, which meant that neither the athletic director nor I needed to help out for lunch periods. This, hopefully, is a sign of good things to come....

Because my midday was clear, this gave me a rare opportunity to set up some formal observations with teachers. I reached out to four of them to see what their plans were in an effort to find a day and a class period that would work into my schedule for the observation process. I felt that while we had significantly fewer cases of the virus and with greater adult attendance in the building (at least for now!), I had better take advantage of this opportunity and schedule what I could.

Continuing with the ***positive***... We had good reports from our

Homecoming Dance that was held Saturday after the boy's basketball game. While the virus cases had been high the past week or so for students as well as staff, we decided that we really needed to continue with the dance plans just as we have for any sporting events scheduled. Basically, everyone has a choice to make as far as attending or participating. This, at least, is the rationale we have used. More importantly, this dance is the ONLY dance that our students have had in the past two years (other than a very restricted Seniors Only Prom last year), and the students were really excited to have it. There have been far too many events taken from our students these past two years, and it is a contributing factor for the social/emotional/mental state that many of our students are in. For this reason, our students **deserve** to get their normal high school experiences back on the schedule! From what I was told (personally unable to attend because of the college basketball game I attended with my family), the students' reactions while attending the dance spoke volumes!

We also had to follow-up with a severe-weather drill that we missed by being virtual last week. I have had concerns that our new building did not have enough of a "safe zone" to receive all the students (and adults) who would be in that area at any one time. Sure enough, the second-floor students were slowed down in getting in the main first floor hall because of the lack of space available and having to step over first floor students as the second-floor students moved down the hall. This is not going to work! It leaves several of our students in an unsafe stairwell waiting to get to a safe place in an emergency situation when seconds count.

Before anyone got hurt, we decided to seek the advice of the District "Safety Expert" to help us expand the safe zone (based on structural integrity of the building). As I mentioned to the other Apollo administrators as we put our heads together that we needed someone "above us" to make this call! Once we establish a more acceptable safe area for the new building, we could communicate the plan to the teachers/

adults in the new building and have a designated Severe Weather Drill for that section of campus in the very near future. With severe weather months approaching AND especially due to the early December tornadoes that leveled parts of Western Kentucky, we do not need to wait to see this through....

The "Made My Day" moment today was getting to see that "Tommy's" bicycle looked brand-new with the new white-wall cruiser tires that our agriculture students put on for him. I hate that I did not get to see "Tommy" and his reaction when he picked up his bike this afternoon, but my mind and heart tells me that he was grinning ear to ear and that tomorrow he'd be sure to find me.

January 27, 2022 - We have now experienced four days of school this week with positive virus numbers and quarantines steady among staff and students. Other schools in our district are going through a rough time with staff, and DCPS has had another spike in cases among bus drivers. Overall, however, our numbers are currently in a safe place. Hopefully, this means that we can maintain an in-person status for a little while longer!

Since the start of this school year and the move into the new building, some of our students have been confused about where to go when they are called to the office. For the first time in the history of Apollo HS, the front office staff and administrative offices are split and no longer reside collectively at what was previously referred to as the "Front Office." With the new building addition, we now have the Attendance Office to receive students throughout the day as they come and go, to and from off-campus classes. Within this office, the Attendance Clerk, Athletic Secretary, Dean of Students, and In-School Suspension Attendant also reside. Nearby is one Asst. Principal and the School Law

Enforcement Officer (SLEO). Remaining in the Main or "Front Office" is the Principal, the other Assistant Principal, Receptionist, Principal's Secretary, and Bookkeeper.

As you can imagine, since the beginning of the semester on January 4th, students have been showing up at the wrong office. While this has reached a point that most of our students are catching on, some of our students still head in the wrong direction. By the way, the administration team did NOT ask for this! At the point the design team was "at the drawing board" a couple of years ago, we had asked for the entire administration to be kept in the same location (either new building or current location), but we were vetoed by the Board of Ed. We are still working through the new procedures that this set-up has presented us, but we remain unsold on the fact that this will work. It will definitely take some effort on both offices to stay or remain on the same page....

Today I had a handful of meetings that kept my attention (one virtual and one off-campus). The virtual meeting was based on the newly approved state law and understanding for how districts and schools proceed if **_any school_** has to be virtual (because of COVID and the lack of enough adults to function) AND how these expectations are different from a weather-related virtual experience. This is a greatly needed allowance, as districts are currently fighting to stay open and in-person like DCPS did this past week. We are ALL hoping that this new law will not be necessary beyond a couple more weeks. If we are still battling through positive adult cases and active quarantines in mid-February (at the same rate as these past ten days), we are ALL in trouble.

The second meeting was a secondary school and district-level meeting concerning the graduation rate of our students and how the district's collective rate had decreased from 2020 to 2021. All in attendance were in agreement that this decline was a direct result of the conditions we have been working through related to the pandemic. The state graduation rate declined for the very same reason. The issue that has sparked the interest of the board level personnel is the fact that the DCPS rate declined more than the state, and for 2021, DCPS fell below state average. This concern is very understandable.

However, the graduation rate at Apollo HS actually _**increased**_ from 2020 to 2021. This increase, I can safely say, is the direct result of the attention that Apollo HS gave to Summer School 2021 and the numerous adults involved (as well as the numerous students who participated - some for four full weeks!). For the time that I have been principal at Apollo HS, the administrative team plus our senior guidance counselor have been very intentional in our efforts to track down our "Seniors-N-Danger." This process involves the running of failure reports, sitting down to meet as a team, and dividing our list of seniors up to have one-on-one conversations with each student OR conferencing with parents (depending on the level of urgency). This is a time-consuming process but has been pretty effective in getting 95% or more of seniors graduated by the end of June each year.

It is amazing to me the amount of attention given to individual students **_today_** as opposed to when I became an administrator twenty years ago. The biggest difference I have noticed in this time is the lack of a caring adult in the lives of our students. Too many of our students are not being raised by their parents (have foster parents or are living with grandparents/other relatives), or sometimes, completely on their own by the time they are seniors. **VERY FEW** eighteen year-olds in 2022 are ready for that kind of responsibility.

January 28, 2022 (I _MISS_ the students!) - Thankfully, we have spent five full days IN-PERSON this week, despite the continued battle with positive COVID adults and active quarantines. Our district is having issues in only a few schools. Some surrounding districts have reached the same virtual-ONLY status that DCPS had this past week because not enough adults are available to function. Let's all hope that one more week will put the community and region in much bet- ter standing and that we are all able to move forward in-person for the rest of the year! Our students, especially, but also our staff need this very much!

What a difference taking some time away from the school can make for a district in the overall health and well-being of its students and staff. While others are still impacted by the virus in our district, Apollo has maintained a very healthy status among adults to the point that we have had only one adult positive all week until today. This means that we are "firing on all cylinders" with all teachers returning to teaching in classes without covering, cleaning in the building without doubling the amount of space to clean, and preparing/serving food without the need of assistance. This is a TREMENDOUS position to be in...AND, very welcomed!

However, I have to say that "my" students in the Global Fare Line are the interactions that have kept me going most of this past semester. Don't get me wrong, I am happy that we are fully staffed in the cafeteria and conditions have stabilized, preventing the need for any athletic di- rector or principal assistance at the cash register, but I had just gotten used to being close to the students on a near daily basis and miss those interactions dearly. I will just have to look for other means of making these daily connections possible....

Per our weekly task, the leadership team met this morning to discuss several topics. One of the more positive items we settled on involved combining our next Parent-Teacher Conference night with an Open House to let them come in and see our new facilities for the first time. As an added bonus, it is Senior Night for boy's basketball, and we are going to allow FREE ADMISSION as an added gesture of hospitality.

Although Feb. 17 is going to be a very busy day for us at Apollo HS (more on that later), this should be a very **_positive_** experience that connects our community and our parents with our staff. This is a moment that we can re-emphasize the power of **_kindness_**, and that is exactly what my secretary and the bookkeeper set their minds to work on. I am already looking forward to this busy day; the Eagle Family **ALWAYS** comes together and makes events like this **_special_**. Let's just hope that the conditions with the virus AND the weather cooperate!

Another item I made sure to cover was my plan to go through with our mandated Lockdown Drill for the month of January. I am being more sensitive than usual for this practice due to the actual lockdown event that Apollo HS experienced in the minutes leading up to the start of the school day on August 26 of this school year. During this event, the student carrying what turned out to be a VERY real looking BB pistol was contained within seven minutes of the "Lockdown" call over the PA system, but the process of ensuring that this student acted alone took more time (what seemed like hours to everyone in the building) in the "locked down" safe mode (locked classroom doors, in the dark, completely quiet, and out of the view of anyone who might try to look through the window of the door, and… waiting).

As you would expect, there may be some nerves that are still a little raw and sensitive to the thought of that experience on Aug. 26, and even the practicing of the drill may cause undue anxiety. Although the critical importance of exercising these drills speaks for itself, it is not worth putting our students or staff back in that sensitive state-of-mind. Based on this and the discussion among the leadership team, it was decided that I would give explicit instructions on ENL Monday and allow each teacher to follow up with their instructions for what happens in their classrooms to get everyone safe. Later in the week, I would inform the teachers on the morning of the drill that it was coming (so they, at least, could prepare themselves and any anxious students of theirs). Furthermore, the drill would last no longer than ten minutes. Although this may not constitute a "full-fledged" drill as far as the Department of Ed. is concerned, this is all that I intend to put our students and staff through.

This was a tremendous week, and Apollo HS was fortunate to have very few adults out. I am hoping that we pick up next week where we left off....

February 1, 2022 - My hopes have become reality as we have picked up where we left off last week. Numbers of positive cases at not only Apollo HS but also the other schools in our district have stabilized! With this trend, it appears the virus will not be causing us to go into a virtual learning setting anytime soon. This is a great relief to staff, students, AND families!

On the other hand, while the temperature reached over sixty degrees today in our region, we have a winter storm system that does not look good for Thursday and Friday of this week. With this system and declining temperatures, it will start out as rain tomorrow night and could change over to ice before snow. The temperature and the rate it will drop will determine just how much ice, if any. Snow in just about any *typical* amount for our area, we can handle. It's the ice that always scares us and determines the severity of power outages coupled with untravellable conditions in many cases. The Winter Ice Storm of 2009 is the one that none of us want to ever relive. This storm left over a half-million homes without power for several days and killed 24 people in the process. Let's hope that this ice event is more manageable with far less destruction....

Yesterday and today have been two very busy days to start this week. I have done the best I can to connect with the students, considering the "withdrawals" that I mentioned in the last journal entry. The best way to achieve a close connection with students is to be present in the hallways and to visit classrooms. Between these two days, I have had three formal observations where I have spent the entire class period observing a teacher and their students. In these observations, I have affirmed my belief that we have some really good things going on here at Apollo. For two of these teachers, they would easily be considered "Rock Star" status, assuming that there is no experience requirement to acquire such a label (you're right - technically there is not!).

These two young teachers each have their very own strengths that make them special in their own way. What they both have in common is the tremendous ability to establish a warm, nurturing, and judgment-free classroom environment that makes it easy for students to not only participate, but also want to belong. These teachers plan very well and set up their classrooms to provide a very structured and rigorous approach to learning, making the very most out of every instructional minute that they have available. Although I have been a principal for twenty years now and have visited numerous classrooms and provided the best/most candid advice I can offer, I find it very hard to leave these teachers with many, if any, growth opportunities! I am left with the thought that I would love to be a student in their classrooms! THAT is the best compliment that I can give a teacher… Despite what I have detailed in the course of writing/publishing *Humanity in Peril*, there IS hope for education as long as teachers like these two described here are willing to "go the distance"….

The remaining teacher's classroom visit was a pleasant experience as well; however, I just cannot put this teacher in the same category due to this being her intern year. The students in this new program absolutely love the class, and the teacher is a very dedicated and passionate individual. This is a great combination to establish the partnership for a sustainable program. I certainly look forward to seeing this teacher grow, along with her program!

Being out in the building allows me the opportunity to connect with some of "my" Global Fare students. There was one point today that I happened by "Myles," standing there with his leg extended in a pose, showing off one of his shoes to his cronies. I could not help but to comment and say, "Myles, you should have been a model!" At this, "Myles" gives me the "Awe, man!" look while his cronies give an affirming chuckle. "Myles" is one of those students who went through the Global Fare line EVERY day, and I always made a point to interact with him in some way. There are MANY things I will NOT miss about my job by retiring at the end of this year, but I know I will miss connecting with students....

One negative from this busy day was a communication from a parent who complained that there are parents going **_against the direction_** we had asked for with the new drop-off and pick-up procedures. These parents are clogging up the system that we had established (AND had "perfected" down to fifteen minutes for emptying the campus in the afternoon) by dropping off their students in the Student/Staff parking lot. Naturally, these parents are ultimately making it harder on our staff and students to arrive in the morning and leave in the afternoon. Sadly, they may be saving themselves thirty seconds (if any!) by disregarding our instructions for the original system. Today marks the sixteenth day that we have had in-person learning since the semester began, and we already have parents circumventing our efforts to keep **_structure and safety_** at the heart of our pick-up and dismissal process....

One "made my day" moment that made me smile as I walked out of the building to head home on this sixty-degree afternoon, was seeing "Tommy" riding his bicycle with brand-new tires on the sidewalk across the street. It never fails; he always sees me, glances over, and gives me a big wave and smiles as he cruises by...

February 2, 2022 (There IS HOPE for Education) - This day has been all about preparing teachers, staff, students, and families for what to expect tomorrow for the severe weather (ice storm) that is expected in our region. Although the winter storm forecasts so far this winter have been **_way_** off, there is little doubt regarding how much precipitation is headed our way in the next twenty-four hours (over a very large region). With this forecast, temperatures will be dropping from fifty degrees to well below freezing over the same time period. This precipitation WILL FREEZE and/or will be in the form of snow at some point. As a district, it was decided (around noon today) that we would be out tomorrow but would try to continue teaching and learning by exercising a DCPS@Home Day. Let's hope the power outages tomorrow, if any, are kept to a minimum!

The best part of this hectic day was the follow-through on two post-conferences I had with teachers I had recently observed. I wanted to take care of this today due to the likelihood we may not be in person for the rest of this week. Following through with the philosophy that I have carried with me for the better part of my administration, I lean more heavily on the praise and support that the teachers desperately need… **ESPECIALLY** now! Don't get me wrong - I am 100% candid with teachers when they need to work on something or they need to try a new teaching strategy, yet I still feel that it is important to make them feel like a million bucks when you can. Below is what I wrote in the summary of one teacher's observation instrument:

"YOU are a ROCK-STAR!! There IS hope for education as long as we have teachers who:

- **_Connect with students_** and make them feel like they belong and are supported in their learning
- **_Hold students accountable_** in a way that they respect and do not 'push back'…
- **_Think creatively_** and incorporate resources like Maslow's

> Hierarchy with *A Raisin in the Sun* and have students portray the psychiatrist to determine the hierarchy level of the character they choose and WHY??? Absolutely BRILLIANT...!
> - **<u>Treat students with respect</u>** in a manner that they cannot dispute what you are asking them to do.
> - **<u>Follow through with advice</u>**... AND hold true to platforms like SpringBoard for the better good of teaching and LEARNING...
>
> CONTINUE exhibiting these traits that you have and ***do not let anyone or anything put out your flame***. Please keep up the good work!"

There is absolutely nothing sugar-coated about this summary. This teacher deserved this and is on her way to being an exceptional teacher. Education desperately needs teachers like her to stay in the profession **beyond** twenty-seven years. For all the examples that were featured in Book 1, *Humanity in Peril*, I certainly hope that conditions in education are much better twenty-five years from now... and this teacher is not even thinking of retirement!

Another event that made this day special for me was the invitation to speak to our EDU 201 (Introduction to Education) class, taught by an exceptional Apollo teacher. Surpassing "Rock Star" status is not the common feat that you may be thinking - just to clarify that these are NOT titles I give **every** teacher. Regardless, who better to teach, mold and instill passion in ***potentially*** future educators than an exceptional teacher?

In the twenty-five minutes that I had with these students, I painted the picture for them of the conditions that teachers are working in. I let them know that it was hard to find teachers, especially in certain subject areas, **before** the pandemic. I told them the advice I had recently given my daughter, Lauren, as she is student-teaching and how she should make herself "marketable" and how it was important to "look" and "act" like a teacher. I answered the questions that the students asked, holding nothing back, because it is critically important that these students know what they are getting into! Yes, these students need to know (for example) that dealing with parents is the hardest part of the job (it is, at least in my humble opinion!).

The last message I left with these "glimmers of hope" was for them to stop at **_nothing_** in their desire to become teachers. Education needs them, and the future of humanity depends upon the hiring of good teachers in the near future! I also told them that I can foresee better conditions by the time that they graduate from college and get their certifications. While I do not know this for certain, something **must change** for the better (again, the **very reason** I have written and published these books!) or the end result will be disastrous....

The best part of my visit to the EDU 201 class was seeing all but three students raise their hand when I asked if they felt certain about pursuing education. This left me feeling pretty good as I traveled home in the rain that would be turning into ice within a twelve-hour period. Yes, there IS hope...

February 4, 2022 - Although the Apollo HS housing boundary suffered some power outages that we all felt were imminent, overall we escaped the level of icing that was forecasted yesterday. For anyone (like my wife and me) who lived further east, very little icing at all occurred and most of the precipitation received in this storm came down in the form of rain. We are VERY thankful that the temperature stayed above freezing for as long as it did. Otherwise, this winter storm could have very easily produced the same catastrophic damages that the 2009 Ice Storm did. Yes, VERY thankful...

Yesterday "counted" as far as a school day is concerned, and it would not have to be made up before the end of the year. Unfortunately, it did NOT count as any worthwhile teaching or learning experience because of the number of students who either **_did not_** log in to Google Meets or **_could not_** log in because they had sketchy internet service or no electricity because of a power outage. Some of our teachers didn't have power by mid-day, while others do not have powerful enough Wi-Fi service to pull off Google Meets under normal conditions. Yesterday was a wash that "counted" as far as the calendar is concerned, but it was far from a day where any meaningful learning took place. Education, in my opinion, needs to move away from the use of NTI (Non-Traditional Instruction) days, unless it is an extreme circumstance. All we have done with what took place yesterday (not just in Daviess County, but in **_any_** of the surrounding counties in our region) was shorten the school calendar by one day....

Regardless of yesterday, TODAY was a traditional "snow day" for DCPS, where most of our neighbors made it another NTI Day. Considering families in a widespread area are dealing with power outages today, Daviess County made the **_correct call_**, and I strongly feel that the other districts in our region should have followed suit. But, then again, that is not my concern....

For today, even though it was a traditional "snow day," I had asked that the Leadership Team at least be prepared to log in to a Google Meet for our weekly Leadership Meeting because we had some important things coming up over the next two weeks. I was hoping that everyone could spare thirty minutes or so today so that we would not have to fit a Leadership Meeting on a Monday returning from an extended absence. All but our instructional coaches joined in on the Google Meet that lasted about thirty-five minutes.

In our short virtual meeting, we discussed the issue with our parents who are causing issues by going against our system for pick-up in the afternoon and the need for our School Law Enforcement Officer (SLEO) to be present for dismissal starting Monday. We also discussed the status of some of our seniors and the upcoming week being a designated "check-in" with an updated failure report. We also made preparations for the special Open House and Parent-Teacher Conference on February 17 and the fact that we were having issues with "punch-list" construction items that **should** have been taken care of weeks ago. Still yet, the embarrassment of our parents and community coming in to see our new state-of-the-art facility and seeing a leaking brand-new water fountain, or… worse yet, using a restroom and noticing that the toilet they used would not flush properly were nightmares we did not want to see come true. Needless to say, we **all** agreed these items must be taken care of well before February 17!

The meeting today also included a discussion of what our scheduling process would look like and a very unofficial glimpse into what our 2023 staffing allocation would be. This unofficial number has typically already been shared (by the end of January at the latest) so that we can start planning accordingly. For whatever reason, this process has been delayed slightly, making it hard for us to see what decisions we need to make to prepare for the 2023 school year. Hopefully, the preliminary allocation report will be coming to me by the end of next week as promised in a conversation I had with the DCPS Secondary Schools Director.

Being that I did not want to tie up the Leadership Team any more than necessary (all were at home except for me!), we ended our meeting after thirty-five minutes. At the very least, we had the important dis- cussions we needed for events coming up, and it eliminated the need for setting aside time on Monday to gather when we are trying to "restart" at the beginning of the week. After the meeting was over, I finished up a few items and gathered my belongings to head home. I hope that these virus and weather interruptions are going to come to an end soon - just so we can maintain consistency and finish our year on a positive note!

February 7, 2022 - The "restart" after a severe weather event is always challenging enough. When the restart is on a Monday, that looks and feels like a Monday, it makes it even harder. It is a good thing that we went ahead with the Leadership Team Meeting this past Friday because we would not have had time to fit it in this morning. Too many challenging events that happened prevented any attention given to anything else.

A student re-enrolled at Apollo today after being sent to an "institution" for the past 45 school days. You would think that spending that much time in an "institution" would have some positive effect on the student and prepare them for a safe and productive return to their home school; however, it RARELY works that way, and today was a perfect example.

This student was only present today for two full class periods when he had very inappropriate words with his 3rd period teacher (who was only trying to get him to come inside the classroom without being tardy). The end result was this student being suspended, pending a hearing based on the words that he used and his actions afterward. He basically informed the administrators who processed him that "it didn't matter what school they put [him] in, [he was] going to run away...." With the help of our SLEO, the administrators were able to process him and get this student out of the building. It's a wonder that this student didn't hurt himself or someone else in the process....

As I mentioned in *Humanity in Peril*, we have had concerns for the mental health of our students even before this pandemic started in the late winter of 2019. The pandemic has only made this concern and the conditions of some of our students even worse. Albeit a small population of our student body, there are about two-to-three percent of our students who have no place in the regular school setting. This student who re-enrolled today is a perfect example. Sadly, the reason that the student returned is more than likely related to the guardian's insurance reaching a maximum coverage, and as a result, the Department of Juvenile Justice (DJJ) decides that the best setting for the student is to return back to their home school.

This is yet another problem that education is facing. The DJJ feels that they have no other recourse but to place students like this back in schools, which is a very dangerous situation that happens far more than the public realizes and is a cause for concern. Because of the growing concern for the mental health of some of our students, the government must provide alternative learning centers with overnight living potential. If this is not done at least at a regional capacity (**_doubling_** what may already exist), students like this very young juvenile will only become a statistic. It is only a matter of time before this student makes a very poor decision and someone gets hurt....

The next most troubling item that I had to work through today was our issue with parents who have completely sacked our pick-up process in the afternoon from what we had communicated at the beginning of the year. Now that there are no adults present in the parking areas (administrators and maintenance personnel), a good handful of our parents are picking up their sons and daughters anywhere they please (as it was relayed to me by our SLEO). The problem? Mass congestion and the mixing of students and parents in the same area as opposed to our system we had established that kept parents, students, and buses completely separated. What a mess, and what a shame!

I reached out to the people that could help in this situation (superintendent, architect, director of maintenance, etc.) and asked for their help and guidance. The one item that would correct this issue is constructing another entrance into our student parking lot. For now, there is only one entrance which forces students leaving and parents entering into close proximity. If a second entrance were added, we could designate one to be for parents and one to be for students. Naturally, this option will only cost money, and it is likely not going to be taken care of any time soon. All I can do is ask… In the very least, I will look forward to the advice from anyone that I sent the email to with any form of help or guidance for this issue….

Ending this journal entry on a positive note - we had ONE teacher out of the building today, only because of jury duty! It has been a LONG time (maybe since the first week of the school year) we have had all but one teacher present for work. Although I am not sure yet what our student attendance was, I venture to say it was better today than any day since Christmas Break. Let's hope this trend continues…!

February 9, 2022 (On the *OTHER* hand…) - I have spent the most part of Book 1 and this book spotlighting teachers who are "Rock Stars" or "Dynamos," and I have pumped up teachers in general for the work they have been doing over the past couple of years. Let's not forget the respect that educators deserve that I have asked for communities and politicians to consider. YES, educators and the schools they work in most definitely NEED and DESERVE support. Teachers ARE professionals and should be treated as such…!

On the ***other*** hand, there are times that I have been disappointed by the lack of attention given to teacher tasks over the years by more of these ***professionals*** than I should. To be fair, I can only speak for Apollo HS, and maybe this is not a nationwide issue. However, I venture to say that a small number of teachers in ***every school*** exist who have developed bad habits and are not organized enough to follow through with "teacher tasks" that come with the job.

The biggest issue I have seen among teachers these past three years (even before the pandemic began) is lack of adequate grading and entering grades into the Student Information System (SIS) gradebook to give an accurate picture student progress. To give an example of this, as of Monday of this week (Day 25 of the semester), fifteen percent of our teachers had at least one class that had **ZERO** grades entered in the gradebook!?! How can this be?? To dismiss grading and entering grades in the gradebook is an integral part of the job! To dismiss grading for that long of a period would be the same as an employee at Subway deciding they were just going to focus on making sandwiches and NOT take part in the cleaning up during or afterward. The difference between these two scenarios is that after skipping out on cleaning a couple times, the Subway employee is likely to be fired.

As administrators, we have the unfortunate displeasure of hovering over teachers like this to make sure that they are entering grades so that students and parents have an accurate measure of student progress. To be honest… with all of the distractions that we have to deal with on a daily basis, we really don't have time to fully attend to holding these teachers accountable… and WHY SHOULD WE? I contend that teachers NEED to act like the professionals that they are and administrators should not have to take time to make sure items like this are taken care of….

Deep breath… Count to ten… But then again, we ARE talking about *fifteen* percent of the faculty with this issue. This means that eighty-five percent are, at least, entering grades and likely sixty percent are even entering grades **weekly**. As the principal, it is your job to focus on the fifteen percent, whether you like it or not… whether you have **TIME** to or not! Because of all the distractions and other parts of your job as a principal, this is a **challenge** to take care of. There are definite times in my administrative career that I have failed to meet this challenge.

This afternoon, we had a faculty meeting to address this issue. Tomorrow, I will be asking the two assistant principals to address this issue further with any of the teachers that they evaluate, and it will be based on a grading report from the guidance office.

———————◆———————

Moving on.! I have to point out something very positive that has occurred today– for the first time since October. We had ZERO positive cases for the virus among students and staff! It is hard to believe that just three weeks ago, the adults were struggling to survive based on the number of teachers who tested positive or were otherwise quarantined. This trend couldn't have happened at a better time! Adding to this, the extended weather forecast shows above forty-degree temperatures for the next several days with not much chance of precipitation, if any. We have HOPE to maintain in-person learning as long as both of these trends continue....

February 11, 2022 - Some days just "line up" with events that have your head spinning as an administrator. Today was one of those days, and my head was spinning before noon. SEVERAL meetings that all landed on the same day, with a parent meeting before the school day started, and a parent meeting after the day was done. In between, some meetings that I had set up on my own and students who chose to come to see me today, for various reasons, also filled my schedule. I did not dare turn anyone away (especially the students!), but it sure seemed that I had a month's worth of meetings all in the same day....

In one of our meetings today, we resolved a conflict and miscommunication that occurred earlier in the week about a student who was questioned about what they were wearing. The initial explanation or question was whether the clothing had anything to do with gang attire. Upon further notice and looking into (unfortunately **_after_** the student had gotten upset and had parent permission to go home) was that the clothing had more to do with supporting their heritage and was completely appropriate. Although I was completely caught off guard and disappointed when this student told me what she wears shouldn't be "white man's business(!)," this meeting today led to a positive conclusion.

The administrators involved in the incident occurring earlier in the week and I found out what upset this student the most. When the administrator saw this student from a distance across the lunchroom, he asked a nearby minority employee (who works in the discipline office) to confront the student about what they were wearing. This is something that we administrators do all the time, especially in times like these when students are super-sensitive to WHO is talking to them (sending a female to speak to a female or sending someone who "connects" better with a student, etc.), AND, we certainly do this with the best intentions!

However, as it turns out, this student saw this as the administrator TREATING her or bringing attention to her as a MINORITY student. The student felt that if **HE** wanted to confront her about it, he should have done so himself, AND if he had, he would be treating her just like any other student at Apollo! Whether this would have been the case or a better solution is still yet to be tested, I can certainly see the point that the mother and student were making… and it is not something I would have ever thought of until they just mentioned it.

Now, I also realize that this type of approach is not at all "universal" to be considered to work for ALL students and ALL cultures. However, it highlights the complexity of the approaches that administrators today have with diverse student populations. Notes taken in the back of my mind today… don't you worry! I will continue to see where this relationship between the student and administration goes….

Picking up from Wednesday's journal entry and the professional responsibilities of our teachers, I had a conference today with one of the teachers I highlighted in Book 1, *Humanity In Peril*.

If you read that book, you will recognize a teacher that I described to be a phenomenal bell-to-bell teacher who had a tremendous knack for not only connecting with students but also finding the most unique and innovative ways to connect the content and skills in a way that the students can completely understand.

The issue is that this teacher is overwhelmed due to having far too many "irons in the fire" and also is a little scatter-brained (organizationally) with a touch of self-admitted ADHD (Attention-Deficit Hyperactivity Disorder). Putting it bluntly, this teacher cannot keep grades up and get them entered in the gradebook for students and parents to see. I fumed over this Wednesday (as my journal entry attests), and yesterday, I was fully preparing in my mind to bring him in today and "put my foot in his rear"! [Please understand that this statement has nothing to do at all with a "physical" interaction, but the same effect as a completely VERBAL interaction with another individual. It comes from my days as a coach, and those who know me **well** have probably heard the more colorful version of the statement….]

Our meeting started with my knowledge that this teacher was not at all happy and that I am not the only one who has noticed it. This person is not the same person who walked our halls two years ago, and you can read the anguish on his face, at least when he is not teaching.

I expressed my concern for him continuing (by his own plan) teaching after this year at Apollo HS.

He fully admitted he was not happy. He was overwhelmed, felt his classroom gets interrupted too many times in a class period, and he cannot keep his head above water with everything else that is going on. This teacher is a tremendous coach and puts one-hundred percent into his programs and athletes. I explained to him (as I have on other evaluative occasions) that this CANNOT continue to happen. He has opportunities with the people he works with on his coaching staff, and he has opportunities with the adults he has within his classroom to GET HELP.

In the course of this conversation (even more so than a similar conversation we had earlier in the year), I determined that this teacher is very close to the "edge." To make myself very clear in what I was trying to tell him, I asked, "If NOTHING changes about how things are going for you (feeling overwhelmed and **_unhappy_**), where do you see yourself this time next year?" The answer was obvious and on the verge of emotion... "NOT in a good place."

I tried my best to use this point as leverage and explain that I would have no choice but to "fire" him as a coach so that he could focus on his teaching duties. While I am saying this, fully understanding THIS IS NOT WHAT NEEDS TO HAPPEN AT ALL, still, this very thought left an impression. I asked this teacher to do some soul searching and "outside-the-box" thinking and find some **_solutions_** to the problem. If the solution to this problem wasn't going to come from either one of us, WHO would it come from? I asked him if he had been passing on an offer from someone who works with him in the classroom to help with his grading and grade entering? Head down... too proud to relinquish this part of his teaching that puts him the "master" of his domain, the look on his face gave me signs of acknowledgement. I went further to say that I would even secure funds for the rest of this year to find someone who could take on his managerial duties as a coach so that he could focus solely on the COACHING of his athletes and not consume more of the available time that he has in a 24-hour day.

The last comments that I gave this teacher were these: I am going to be VERY disappointed to hear that you have retired after twenty-seven years. Education NEEDS this teacher to retire after thirty-two years (the "old" version of this teacher that we all knew and appreciated started coming out at this point as he tried to negotiate for thirty years instead). STOP passing up on the "Rock Star" support that you are being offered, and FIX this problem! I DO NOT want to be in this same conversation at ANY point next year! He realized that these words I gave him had to come true and that HE had to take action. What normally would have been a handshake and a "make it happen" closure to our discussion became a "bro-hug" at his request. As we hugged, I delivered the "MAKE IT HAPPEN" message, and he went out my office door and on his way....

There IS hope for education if THIS teacher is still teaching after thirty years. I happily shredded my mind's formal reprimand that wasn't in print form yet. Don't think for a second that I will not be following up on the items that this teacher needs to MAKE HAPPEN....

February 14, 2022 - As I mentioned in Book 1, I do not take time off very often. Over thirty-two years in education, I cannot recall using more than ten sick days or the same for personal days. Based on the "overtime" that I worked over Christmas Break making sure that the move into the new building went well, I have been granted the ability to get some of that time back. Today is one of those days, and it couldn't have been more well spent....

Over the course of this past weekend, I was able to visit with my oldest son, Todd, as well as share some time with my second oldest son, Troy, who had traveled home for Super Bowl Weekend. It is such a pleasure to connect with your adult children, as they explain the latest events that have taken place in their busy lives. It is hard not to picture their 4-year old selves sitting in front of you as they relay what has transpired in their world. It is truly a full-circle moment as a parent that makes you proud. Despite the issues that they may be challenged with, they are finding their way and making decisions that will keep them moving forward, prospering and making an impact in their "neck of the woods." For both Todd and Troy, I informed them of my retirement at the end of the year and the publishing of Book 1, *Humanity in Peril*, with hopes that they could understand AND appreciate my purpose in making my work public....

Today was spent traveling to Lexington with Angela and our youngest son, Aaron, to see Lauren and take her out to eat for an in-person Valentine's Day treat. Lauren is going through student teaching at an elementary school in Fayette County, and it is always a blast to hear her talk about her experience. To have our daughter speaking in a language that only educators would understand and appreciate is a gratifying moment for this career educator! I also shared with Lauren my intent to retire at the end of this year, along with my book writing. Although my bones don't travel as well as they used to, the six hours spent on the road was worth every moment that we were able to spend with her. Again, it was the moments pictured below that I had on my mind as we were lost in discussion with Lauren and her student teaching experience (I framed this drawing of Lauren's from when she was five years old and had left me a note attached in her own five-year old language, saying, "Dear Dad, I hope we go camping"). This day with Lauren was just as special as the days that the kids and I spent camping next to the lake on our small farm. There is **_nothing at all_** that I could have achieved on this level by being at work today!

February 15, 2022 (The downside…) - Just to be certain, I wouldn't change the time I had yesterday spent traveling to see Lauren and find out the latest from her world; however, the one reason that I have rarely missed over the years is the work that you have to come back to any time you are absent. This week was already slated to be a very busy week at Apollo. Being out yesterday typically means that I will have five days of work to do in four.

This morning started out following this pattern as individuals approached me about needs from yesterday. We also had three of our ATIP (Apollo Teacher Intern Program) Cycle 2 meetings for three of our interns scheduled today. These meetings involve four of us veteran educators (Mentor Teacher of the same content, Instructional Coach, District Specialist, and Administrator) discussing the growth of the intern, the strengths the intern has displayed, and the growth opportunities that we feel they should focus on moving forward. These discussion points are based on what each of us have observed in the intern's classroom. Once the intern joins us for the discussion, it is very positive and supportive of their growth since the beginning of the year, and it is supportive for their work on growth items moving forward. I thoroughly enjoy being a part of these meetings and the discussions that unfold. For the most part, Apollo has been blessed with interns showing tremendous potential from the start. Surrounding them with four veterans is the least we can do to support them... MORE evidence that there IS hope for education...!

Most of the rest of this day was a blur, and the vast majority of my time seemed spent inside my office. Apollo HS has an Accreditation Review visit over the next two days that will involve a team of four individuals interviewing students, parents, community members, leadership, support staff, etc., as well as a review of documents we have provided them prior to the visit. These visits typically happen every five years or so, but because of the pandemic, this process has been delayed by a couple of years. Ultimately, it has been around seven years since Apollo HS had their last visit (this is my sixth year at Apollo HS).

Overall, I have no anxiety that would normally come with hosting one of these visits because the leadership team (mainly one of the "Dynamo" instructional coaches) has laid the foundation for what is needed for the visits. More importantly, despite the challenges that we are facing at Apollo HS this year and what we endured last year, I very much believe in the daily work and grind at our school. The biggest challenge regarding this visit and interviews is that it will be a 100%

virtual experience! Not only will this be very awkward, but I suspect that virtual visits by individuals who know very little about your school will be about as effective as what we have found virtual instruction to be. Whether this will be found true or not will be revealed at the conclusion of the process when the review team presents their findings. Either way, we have little control....

One thing did catch my attention today with all the busy tasks that consumed me. At one point just after lunch, one of our "Dynamo" instructional coaches had shared with me that one of our teachers had to be relieved of her classroom because she was very distraught due to a negative experience with one of her students. One of our administration team members had to monitor her classroom while she "took a moment."

As I always try to do, I follow through with these requests because the support team I have around me would not ask if it weren't necessary. The first opportunity I had was within ten minutes after the dismissal bell sounded. The teacher was guiding a student with a project they were working on for class. The teacher noticed me at her door and asked if I needed her. I just asked her if she was OK. At this, she started tearing up again, but she said that she was going to be OK. I didn't want to compound the issue by pressing further (especially with the student present), but I told her that I am available if she needed any support.

While I have not mentioned it as much as I did in the journal entries that make up *Humanity In Peril*, I am still very concerned about the behavior of our students and days like this that put our teachers "in a bad place." Whatever was said or done in this teacher's class was unfortunate and unnecessary. The collection of these types of events are what jeopardizes our teaching force moving forward. I intend to find out more details, just to be sure whatever discipline that was necessary was effectively and appropriately applied, if nothing else.

February 17, 2022 - Wednesday was a blur as the leadership team and a few groups of teachers/staff members were interviewed virtually by the accreditation team. Throughout the day, the team would ask for an item or two of evidence that we had not provided them before the "visit" started. This is the fourth accreditation visit that I have been a part of as a principal, and it is always comforting to get the first day behind you.

Today involved mostly student interview groups, and we had arranged for a very heterogeneous grouping of students to include "all walks of life" here at Apollo HS. The instructional coach "Dynamos" did an exceptional job setting this up to include an extra group of English Learners (EL) as well as one group of EL parents (parents who would not struggle with the language barrier). Because these visitors are not on site for us to support if they need anything, we can only hope that everyone (students and parents) makes it to their virtual interview time with no troubles. That is something we will find out tomorrow. All in all, the day seemed more "normal" because I was not involved with any of the interviews and was not contacted by any of the review team members.

Today was a very BIG day at Apollo HS; not only did we have Day 2 of the accreditation "visit," but we also had Parent-Teacher Conferences that led into an Open House for our community to tour our new facilities for the very first time, topped off with our last home boy's basketball game, which also included Senior Night and free admission for all! HUGE day in the "Big A!" While offering these opportunities for our parents and community, we are modeling and supporting the "Be Kind" initiative that our district is sponsoring this month.

Because of the events scheduled today, I got more steps in than usual, as I made trips to several different areas to check on cleanliness and also our new addition. While making my rounds, I stopped by the Media Center to make sure our students who were helping us through the accreditation review process were arriving on time and were where they were assigned. For one of the groups, I retrieved one of the students who obviously does not read emails regularly and delivered her to the Media Center. Seeing that the "Dynamos" had this process VERY much under control (as always!), I moved on to check on some other items on my list.

One of many AWESOME reasons to be a principal involves the moments that you find yourself at the right place, at the right time. Because of my coverage as a cashier to help the shortage of cafeteria staff the first semester, the lunch ladies go **_further_** out of their way to take care of me. Today was one of those lucky days for me!

As I started to pass through the Commons Area where our ladies were eating (prior to serving student lunches), one of them stopped me to say I needed to get one of the **_hot, just out of the oven_** cinnamon rolls! Just as soon as she mentioned it, the smell hit me, and BOY, I could not bring myself to turn the offer down! What a treat... followed by a fresh cup of coffee! While I normally watch what I eat and pass by sweets like this, I **_had_** to oblige today. My weigh-in tomorrow morning will not be what I will be hoping to see. Maybe the extra steps I am taking today will allow me to work off those calories... DOUBTFUL....

The afternoon quickly spilled over into a presentation to the Daviess Co. Board of Ed. And back to Parent-Teacher Conferences at Apollo, where I tried to make my way around to get an idea how many parents joined us. Nearing the end of the conferences, I also had an opportunity to deliver one of the parents to a teacher located in the new building (it was far easier to escort her than to try to explain the many turns and steps it would take to get her there!). The Open House allowed us the opportunity to see some community members and some of our most recent retirees who wanted to see what the new space looked like. All-in-all, the Open House was a hit, and it allowed more people to attend the basketball game who normally would not have considered joining us for such events. In the end, fifty-two visitors joined us for the Open House, in addition to the parents who signed up and participated in conferences; unfortunately, the Eagles lost to visiting Christian County in front of THE biggest crowd Apollo has seen in over two years....

February 18, 2022 - It sure has been a LONG week, especially considering I had Monday off! This week culminated into a deep discussion in our weekly leadership meeting regarding our recent release of the ImpactKY Survey results and the completion of our Accreditation Review process with an exit interview this afternoon.

The ImpactKY Survey is a biennial survey given to all certified individuals in each KY school. It is described as a "working conditions" survey, and it focuses on the following areas in the questions that are asked:

- Educating All Students
- Emotional Well-Being and Belonging
- Feedback and Coaching
- Managing Student Behavior
- Professional Learning
- Resources
- School Climate
- School Leadership
- Staff-Leadership Relationships

The questions asked give the certified individuals a range of answer choices, such as, "Almost Always," "Frequently," "Sometimes," "Once in a while," and "Almost Never." Schools are encouraged to get as close to 100% participation as possible, and a non-administrator orchestrates the entire process, ensuring the responses are completely anonymous. The results come back to the school organizer after sixty days or so, and the results are made available to the public a week later.

This 2022 ImpactKY Survey is a hard one to compare to the 2020 survey. While a vast majority of the questions asked are the same, the conditions that teachers are working in are vastly different. To compare, the 2020 version was administered in January 2020, *just before* we knew what was coming with the coronavirus pandemic, the "tsunami" it would represent, and the aftermath we would be working through two years later. EVEN STILL, it is critically important that the leadership of a school wraps minds around the results and looks for solutions to make conditions better.

I had the distinct pleasure of being asked to serve on the KDE Working Conditions Steering Committee with about fifteen other professionals in October 2019. It was during this steering committee meeting that we "created" the survey and upgraded the questions from the previous TELL Survey process (questions made more simple and drastically reduced number of questions included). It was in this committee meeting that I strongly encouraged them to include the Emotional Well-Being questions, such as, "How concerned are you about your emotional well-being as a result of your work?" This request of mine was made with the **_current conditions at the time_** in mind (teacher shortages, substitute teacher shortages, inadequate pay increases, lack of respect shown by legislators and the governor of Kentucky, etc.) with no knowledge that a coronavirus even existed. Regardless of the before or after pandemic effect, it is very telling to the principal of a school when forty-five percent of your faculty answers "Quite a Bit" or "A Great Deal" to that question. It SHOULD be very telling to the public and legislators....

As a principal of a school, it is easy to feel responsible or even offended by the collective survey results. As a principal of twenty years, I can tell you that I have experienced high and low results and have endured the entire roller-coaster of emotions as I have reflected on them. Over time, I realized that, as principal, I cannot take the results personally, especially in a large school, where it is so hard to understand the perspective of individuals who are answering the questions on the survey. Nevertheless, it is **_THEIR_** perspective, and it is our duty as administrators to take a look at the results collectively, to not only find reasons but especially to seek solutions to the biggest issues that the survey reveals. Like it or not, it is just part of the continuous improvement process....

The leadership team had a good discussion of survey results this morning at our meeting. We all agreed that there are a couple of items that need to be addressed as a result of the survey, but it was important for us to allow the faculty to look over the results and have their own discussions regarding the top areas we want to address as a school. Because this survey represents their voice, the faculty should be instrumental in devising the areas we want to address in an effort to IMPROVE the conditions they are working in. I told the leadership team that we would meet with the Lead Teachers (head teacher of each department) on Tuesday after school, and we would give them the instruction to take the conversation to their department members where the conversations would be more genuine. Within the next two weeks, Apollo HS should have two main focus areas to consider moving forward that we could circle our wagons around in an effort to improve.

This day ended with a virtual meeting consisting of the three-member Cognia Accreditation Review Team, the instructional coach, and me to hear their findings from the two-day visit. Overall, they seemed very impressed with the work we are doing and our efforts to try to improve each year, especially while offering as much support as we can to our diverse student population. The summative score given to us based on a complex rubric of findings through documents shared, interviews, and a review of our processes resulted in a 354 out of 400, which is considered very high for a high school. Within the findings and assessment, they offer us growth opportunities to consider moving forward. The timing of this review process and the ImpactKY Survey is PERFECT, allowing us to consider both sets of feedback to prepare for a better teaching and learning platform heading into next school year....

February 22, 2022 - The beginning and end of this day had me roaming from one end of our stretched campus to the other. I met with one of our ATIP (Apollo Teacher Intern Program) Committees to discuss the progress of our last intern (Apollo has six interns this year) during the Cycle 2 meeting. I always thoroughly enjoy being a part of these conversations because of the very intentional focus that each member brings to the intern's progress and growth. The committee discusses over a twenty-minute period where the intern has experienced the most growth since the Cycle 1 meeting and what we can add to the intern's original list of strengths.

We also discuss the growth areas we feel the intern needs to focus on in order to have the most positive impact on their teaching. When all four of us are doing our part (observing the intern on separate occasions and providing candid feedback), the growth areas seem to materialize out of thin air during our discussion as we enter details on the summary document before sharing with the intern. To me, it is a very powerful process that reinforces unconditional support for the intern teacher. When we need to provide more time to help them, we make time for it to happen. This is one of many things I am proud that we have continued to provide for new teachers/first-year teachers – the Apollo way – simply because it makes a positive impact... AND it is the right thing to do!

Among other post-observation conference meetings I had today with teachers at Apollo, I also had a mid-morning conversation with the superintendent, who wanted to finalize my timeline for closing out my career as a principal at Apollo HS. After a little back and forth, we agreed to accept a timeline that would allow me to remain principal until the end of the year and graduation, at which point the next principal would be announced. This was important to me. I want to be able to work up until the last day of my career without feeling "in the way" or that my time over the last few weeks is wasted. This plan that we discussed should allow me to formally announce my retirement just before spring break and also the announcement of the new principal just before Memorial Day weekend. This timing would allow the new principal the time he/she would need to get adjusted, learn routines/procedures, and get to know leadership staff to develop times for meetings prior to the start of the next school year. Ironically, my first day to report to Apollo HS was exactly one-week before the start of the school year in August 2016....

The last thing that I achieved on this day was meeting with the Lead Teachers to discuss ImpactKY survey results for Apollo HS, the preliminary staffing allocation for 2023, and our plan for scheduling our students for 2022-2023 classes. During this meeting, I explained the process for each department to look over the ImpactKY Survey results. Because nearly 100% of our certified staff answered this survey in the fall, I feel that it is important for all teachers not only to see the results, but to discuss what **_they_** feel are the greatest areas of concern. Within the departments, a greater chance for genuine conversation among members resides; these are the individuals who work closely together on a daily basis. Each department would determine their top three concerns (in priority order), based on their discussion and findings in the Apollo HS 2022 ImpactKY Survey results. The Lead Teachers would then send me their findings to compile and share at the next Leadership Meeting. Ultimately, the hope is that we find a trending top two concerns with some semblance of a direction to start from among the majority of the ten departments within Apollo HS. Departments have one week to get back with me on their findings. I am looking forward to seeing the results of these conversations....

February 23, 2022 - Some days just do not get started on the right foot. TODAY was one of them. Just prior to the school day starting, I tried to see one of our "Rock Star" teachers about some concerns that had recently been communicated, and I could not track the teacher down. Near the same time, I was "cornered" by a parent conversation with a couple of other administrators at Apollo regarding an incident that had occurred this past Friday that required some "further explanation." To be honest, the meeting was not at all necessary, but we had to appease the parents. The end result was that the student in question was NOT being "targeted" by the administration (one of the administrators was his basketball coach) and what Apollo had relayed to the family was 100% protocol for these types of actions by students.

The worst part of this morning was that I had been misguided by some communications from parents regarding the "Rock Star" teacher, and by pulling her out of class to see her and check on her well-being actually backfired on me. It was a mistake on my part, but based on the personal information I had recently been given coupled with the parent's concerns, I felt I needed to check in on this teacher to see if she was in a good place. Again, as soon as my conversation began with her (while the parents of the student in question were still in my office with the two other administrators), I realized that this teacher was just as poised and headstrong as I had ever known her, and it was a mistake for me to pull her from class to engage in this conversation. Sometimes, the BEST intentions come back on you as the principal of a school....

One of the worst parts of being tied down this morning in my office was missing out on my time to share special announcements and birthdays on ENL. A distant second was being late for the district principal's meeting at one of our district office locations. Upon arriving about fifteen minutes late to this meeting, I walked in to find the district principals split into groups and discussing strategic planning for moving forward into a district improvement model. As I tried to get my bearings despite my early morning distractions, there was ONE topic (Retaining High Quality Staff) that lit a fire under me, and I took my turn to share what I had to say.

At the point that it was my group's turn, I stood and unleashed my concerns for the reason that high quality teachers and staff were leaving the profession. EVERY WORD that came together in the creation of *Humanity in Peril* was delivered in the Cliff's Notes verbal version with a little "heat" behind it. Once again, the former coach in me came out, and, yes, I apologized in advance for what I was about to unleash. The negativity within communities, the negativity that was cast on education from our own KY legislators from our past, the lack of adequate cost-of-living increases in pay, AND, I almost forgot, the current conditions that teachers and staff are working through amid this tsunami aftermath IS WHAT KEEPS US FROM RETAINING High Quality Staff! While nobody dared to utter any words of approval, I certainly saw the head nods and the looks on the faces of several principals who acknowledged the "purple elephant" standing in the middle of the room.

The rest of our agenda for the day was wrecked due to the side-bar conversations stemming from my slight derailment. The purpose of our strategic planning as a district was absolutely spot-on and could NOT have been timed more perfectly. The district MUST try to get back in "control" of some of the more concerning issues within education. What the district did not plan for adequately was the amount of time that we needed to discuss our concerns and the "purging" that we needed to take part in (instead of the "dutiful" head-nodding that they normally get in our meetings). This is REAL. The problem needs to be discussed and IDENTIFIED before the district can apply any solutions and especially before strategic planning for improvement....

One LAST item for this day... It is important for me to relay to my readers that there are some items I have endured throughout this year that I have withheld from writing about. Some of the items are so controversial, or so potentially damaging (for me!) that I have had to just keep to myself. One such item happened today (while I was in the process of typing this journal entry), and the irony is the individual involved completely missed the message I was trying to deliver at my "halftime speech" to the district principals, becoming that negative parent with angst fully directed at one of **MY** teachers. On the professional side of education, **ESPECIALLY**, this is something you just cannot do...!

February 25, 2022 (*Anything for the kids...*) - There are times in my tenure as a principal that I have gone to the extreme in support of the staff and especially the students of my school. The communication efforts I have employed have not always been received positively, but the communications have ***always*** been delivered with the ***best interest*** of the school I am leading in mind. Not one of my communications to other leaders in the district was ever personal; it is more about making those who really need to be aware at the district level so that decisions can be made. Bottom line - if I hadn't made those communications in the manner that I did, the conditions I was bringing to the district leader's attention would likely not have changed..., or the conditions likely wouldn't have changed quickly enough. To me, this justifies a good reason for my effort.

This morning was an example of one such communication, and it was delivered straight from my heart. Apollo HS serves as the English-Language (EL) "Newcomer" hub for the district. This essentially means Apollo receives all new enrollees from foreign countries whose primary language is *not* English, regardless of which school zone that the family lives within the county. Within this "newcomer" program at Apollo, students are immersed in learning the English Language and are also taught by EL certified teachers in the core subjects of (English, Math and Science). Adults who receive these students throughout the day are very patient and caring individuals.

Over the six years I have been principal at Apollo HS, we have come a LONG way in our efforts to serve these students! While our EL numbers have grown during that time (the enrollment has more than doubled), we have reached a point that we have an exceptional team in place to meet the daily needs of our students. Don't get me wrong, these students are a **challenge** to have in your school. However, it doesn't take very long for anyone to grow attached to them! The vast majority of these students LOVE being a part of our school, and it can be seen in the way they interact with each other and the adults they are working with. The smiles are the best part – universally accepted acknowledgement that "I am happy" in *any* language....

The unfortunate flaw in our district's procedures is the enforcement of the newcomer students to go back to their "home school" across the county after they have spent two years in Apollo's program. Again, for some students, their family lives out of Apollo's school zone. The problem is that these students have made a HOME at Apollo HS. Through the love and support they have been shown and the connections they have made with other EL students (as well as "regular" students), they do not want to leave. It is painful to know that our dynamic EL team of adults have had to sit down with each of the students who fall into this category and explain to them that they will be going to a different school next year. As you can imagine, these are heartbreaking conversations. Enough is enough... The following is a paraphrase of the communication I sent to those who make EL placement, EL training/ certification, and transportation decisions at the district office:

> All - Please understand that I am sharing this with all of you to make you aware and at the same time to avoid a domino-effect of conversations that would need to take place. This message is coming straight from the heart in an effort to get a procedural/ policy change in regard to our EL program...
>
> Bottom Line - WE LOVE OUR KIDS, and we want what is best for them. In six years, we feel we have finally reached the point that we are making great strides in serving our EL population. There is no way the home school can serve the EL students at the same capacity that we can. This is no disrespect to them, but to consider what we have done in 6 years and the fact that we still have a long way to go in getting our regular teachers trained to support EL students (keep in mind this is our first year of having a full-time EL Instructional Coach), Apollo can still provide much more for these students than their home school. Here are other things to consider in making a decision to allow Apollo to continue serving the EL students who are technically another school's responsibility:
>
> - Our kids LOVE APOLLO and have made a 'home' here! When the EL Team has conversations with them to let them know they will no longer be an Apollo student (because they are exiting the 'newcomer' program), tears flow! One student ran to the restroom crying. One student said that he would just 'quit'. Whether he does this or not, we will see. However, moving kids after they have settled in one school will only increase the chance of dropout....
> - We have families who live in the same household - an example of this are cousins where one student is exiting the newcomer program, and one will stay at Apollo for one more year. The

current policy would put the two kids in two different schools, this will only complicate communication issues we already have with home....

I could come up with more examples, but honestly, this should suffice. The best thing we can do for our EL students in our district is CONSISTENCY, and the best chance of any EL newcomer student completing HS with a diploma is to stay at the same school. Lastly, NOBODY loves our EL kids more than we do at Apollo HS....

Please consider....

ANYTHING for the kids...! I am hoping to find out Monday that this communication was received with the same best intentions it was delivered. I also hope to find out we can cancel the bus trip next week to get these students to visit their new school next year. We will see...,

March 1, 2022 - Some days are just "feel good days" from beginning to end, despite anything negative that may be going on. This day started with a message I delivered to the student body on ENL asking the students, "What is Apollo HS's identity?" Is our identity one of **caring**? Is our identity one of **acceptance**? Do we have **true** school spirit (not just self-proclaimed, but a title others would give us)? Are Apollo students known for **reaching their highest potential**? I encouraged the ENL staff to put together a story on this topic, and I also encouraged the students to ask themselves if they were being responsible.

My reasons for delivering this message to the students were twofold. First, our faculty has expressed concerns for the overall climate of our school based on student behaviors in the recent ImpactKY survey. Second, we have had recent damage in the boys' restrooms in our brand-new state-of-the-art facility, AND our students are leaving horrible messes behind them in the cafeteria during mealtimes. The message I delivered was clear: if we could just be responsible for our own trash, our own messes, and our own behaviors, think about how beautiful our campus (and community) would be?!

"Dynamo" Instructional Coach #1 and I have been in the process of compiling the Top Three ImpactKY survey concerns from our departments around Apollo HS and will be "sorting" and organizing what we receive for us to go into a deeper discussion at the Leadership Team meeting this Friday. Call me crazy, but I always enjoy opportunities to initiate plans to improve in whatever area is needed. As an administrator, when you employ the strategy of involving ALL of your teachers, you have the best chance of getting **near**-complete buy-in from the staff. Change is GOOD, and too many indicators have been revealed (pandemic-driven or not) that Apollo could use a dose or two of GOOD brought on by **team**-driven change....

Today was also the day that our FFA (Future Farmers of America) designated to cook pork chops on the grill and serve the entire staff. Last week was National FFA Week, and this meal has become an Apollo tradition; unfortunately, the weather this past week just wasn't suitable enough.

When this day happens each year, the halls of Apollo HS fill with the smell of pork chops on the grill! The Ag classroom that was designated as the "Eating Hall" was adorned in Mardi-Gras decor (just coincidence that today happens to be "Fat Tuesday"), and many of our staff members spent the first meaningful amount of time in this new area **eating together** for only the fourth or fifth time all-year. Sadly, based on the new teacher eating area being renovated and the fact that the pandemic still has a lot of staff reluctant to share space with their peers, many of our staff eat alone in their rooms. This self-imposed isolation is not any more good for the adults in this building than it was for our students to be isolated this past year. These times that we have **made** opportunities for the staff to eat have come the closest for us to feel like conditions are "normal" again. The smiles and the conversations that fill the air make for a tremendous "feel-good moment" as an administrator....

The **BEST** part of this feel-good day was being asked if I could help cashier at lunch due to four cafeteria workers being absent. This request was not virus related, rather just a day where appointments or other personal needs fell on the same day. Thankfully, I did not have a calendar full of events that had to take place, and I absolutely jumped at the chance! This was my first opportunity to interact with the students in the lunch line since the third week in January. As I have mentioned before, even though Apollo has five serving lines to choose from, most of our students are creatures of habit and report to the same line EVERY day. "Where have you been, Mr. Lasley? We missed you!" as well as other bantering comments delivered to certain students made me feel like I was home after a long journey. Seeing many of the same faces again (remembering a good number of their names) and engaging in friendly conversation again was just what I needed! This encounter also allowed me to check in on a couple of students who had recently fallen into some "hard times." Just the acknowledgement from them that "things are going better now" was the icing on the cake of this feel-good day....

Last item for today -- the last-ditch effort communication that I sent out at the end of the week to try to keep our EL students from moving to another school has given us reason to put the field trip visit to their "new" school on pause. I feel strongly that the district is looking at the best interests of these students and may allow them to stay. Whether transportation will actually be provided is another story, but we will take "pause and a consideration" as a small victory for now....

March 3, 2022 - Today was another LONG and busy day at Apollo HS, but one that had several good moments. Five members from Central Office paid a scheduled visit to follow me into some classrooms for observations. Just before one of the class periods started while my guests and I were waiting in the hall, one of Apollo's well-known "radar" kids started walking towards the superintendent and me with a curious look on his face (he took notice of the man in the suit and tie). "I have a suggestion…," he started. "Why is it such a big deal for us to wear hats? I can understand the hoods, but why hats?" After hearing him out, I explained that we were looking into making some changes to the student dress code for next school year, and I wrote him a note to get to his classroom. Knowing that this student is always on the administration's radar, I knew his teacher would not accept his being tardy to class without a note.

The funniest part of this confrontation was that this student approached the superintendent as if he were the captain of Apollo's debate team; he's a very shrewd wordsmith who knows the proper tone and sophistication to ask questions in an effort to persuade a certain response. Our superintendent *may* have been impressed, but I made sure to let him know that this kid was full of bologna…!

The five observations went smoothly during our first collective walk-through experience in the new building. As the central office team and I went room to room, we jotted down some notes that we could each reflect on together after the experience was over. I made sure to leave a large post-it note with feedback and one suggestion for the teacher as we exited. I have found that if I do not take time to do this at the moment, I have a hard time following through with **ALL** teachers I visit. Too many times, something will inevitably "get in the way," and I feel guilty because I have shared feedback for some teachers and not others. Some administrators would have a hard time with this process and would likely have a better way to provide a two-way system of reflection. This process is one that I have found works for me, and I know I can at least be **consistent**.

Once the central office team departed, I made an opportunity for the "Dynamo" Instructional Coach and me to sit down and go over the feedback that we received from each of our eleven department lead teachers. This feedback was based on the ***genuine*** discussions that came from each department as they interpreted the ImpactKY survey data and prioritized a list of top 3 concerns they felt Apollo needed to address.

What we quickly determined was that nearly all of our departments identified the same three concerns but may have had them in a different priority order. We decided that Student Behavior was the #1 concern, followed by Educating ALL Students. The greatest impact for any work to improve these areas to directly affect our Culture and Climate as a by-product. Consensus was reached without much effort, as we both read very similar trends and messages within the feedback. We spotlighted three distinct tasks that needed to be handled and the leaders who would be responsible for seeing each task through. The administrators would tackle an overhaul of our discipline code with one member of each department being a part of the work. The end result would be the most refined list of all the "battles" that we **ALL** agree are the ones worth fighting, along with the agreement (signatures in "blood," if needed) to hold **ALL** of our students accountable. The instructional coaches would seek input to prepare for summer training for our teachers to have confidence in having the awkward conversations that we have avoided these past two years with our students and also ways we can address the equity in the education of our students. The last task was all mine, and it involved following through with personnel decisions that had become apparent barriers to the mission we make an effort to live by at Apollo HS. We left our meeting fully prepared to share with the rest of the Leadership Team tomorrow at our weekly meeting.

Hands down the BEST part of this day involved the energy around the building that was coming from the impromptu preparations that

I had initiated by asking our pep adult and student leaders at Apollo to make our FIRST school-wide pep rally in over two years happen TOMORROW. Yes, while normally we like to plan these out more in advance, it wasn't until we witnessed our E-gals basketball team advance in the regional tournament in Apollo fashion that we came up with the idea that it was time to gather in this assembly. This pep rally would not just be about our E-gals, but it also would be more inclusive of all our teams who have recently competed at state and national levels and WON, as well as teams we have going next week to compete as well. Regardless of ANY reason, this energy being felt all over the building was LONG OVERDUE. The drastic reduction of positive virus cases within the community over these past two weeks could not have come at a better time....

The only "downer" experience for today was the lack of participation that we had among our families for our traditional scheduling fair. I have always been impressed with the sheer number of parents (especially incoming 9th grade parents) who would join us along with their child for this after school event to sit down with a faculty member and walk through the process to schedule their child's classes for the up-coming school year. The pandemic has put a halt to this tradition these past two years, and we were hoping to resurrect it this year. What had been as much as eighty-five percent participation of freshmen parents in the past was closer to twenty-five percent participation tonight. A very quick summation for the reasons that this may be the case led us to the fact that the on-line process for setting this up at the middle school level is much easier, and there is very little clean-up needed. Let's hope that the lack of participation for this event has more to do with this than any avoidance from our parents....

March 4, 2022 - Today was one of the more busy Fridays that we have had in a while after a very busy week. The Leadership Team had to condense our meeting into a shorter amount of time due to another meeting I had to be present for at Central Office. We just had enough time to discuss our feelings about the Scheduling Fair and the potential reasons for parents not showing up, the two focus areas that the instructional coach and I had surmised from the department ImpactKY feedback, and the staffing additions that we **may be** considering for the start of next school year. Despite the lack of time to go into much depth, the items discussed were made pretty clear, and the team indicated they could see the reasons for the two focus areas that needed our attention. Having no time to join in on the idle chatter and banter that takes place as we end our meetings (or at the beginning), I sped in the direction of Central Office....

One of the most *awesome* aspects of being a part of the high school experience is the events that make the high school experience unique. Clubs, extra-curricular activities, athletics, and any event that makes today's students into tomorrow's leaders are the more pleasurable to witness and be part of as an educator. The incredible stature of our students and how they develop as leaders through the guidance and tutelage of the adults who surround them in high schools is a spectacle that *still moves me* after thirty-two years in education. To me, NOTHING compares to the high school experience....

This week ended with **THE** most incredible and spirited pep rally I have witnessed in my career. Considering the short notice I gave the pep sponsors when I asked if we could put this together, this pep rally was a true marvel to behold! What made this pep rally special was that it was the first school-wide pep rally in over two years at Apollo because of the pandemic. The last pep rally that took place was October

2019 or earlier! Our 9th and 10th grade students have never had the experience of a HS pep rally... until today.

While our younger students walked in the gymnasium without really knowing what to expect, our juniors and seniors embraced this opportunity. It was as if the energy from all the lost pep rally events over these past two years was bottled up and kept dormant within each student, only to be released collectively at this precise moment. The looks on the faces of every adult in attendance, the students standing and participating (like I have never witnessed before!), the creative design of our adult and student leaders, and the ENERGY we all experienced the last thirty minutes of this school day brings a little moisture to my eyes as I type these words. YES! For this small moment we all shared, it felt as if the pandemic NEVER happened!

My clumsy words cannot begin to do justice for what we witnessed this afternoon:

March 7, 2022 (*Insignificance…*) - Sometimes, the role of principal in a high school is an emotional roller-coaster. You go from the "high" experience that we had at Apollo with the pep rally at the end of the day Friday to the "low" that I experienced today. Despite every effort you make to be a positive influence to correct something in the best interest of students, there are days that your influence just wasn't enough. On this dark, cold, dreary, rainy day, my mood seemed to follow the weather; it's days like this that I do my best to remain in my office and have little contact. There is plenty of documentation for teacher and staff evaluations or other desk-work that can be found. The following describes events from today that fed into my mood:

This morning prior to the school day beginning, one of our students who is seen frequently around the building wearing his hood walks by as he takes his hood down. As I mentioned to him to keep his hood off today, I saw him out of the corner of my eye pulling his hood back up over his head as he was heading to his first period class. Despite the numerous times I have mentioned this as a safety issue on ENL (hoods prevent us from easily identifying students either "live" or especially on grainy video footage) and the administrators helping reinforce this with every student they see, there are students like this one who will continue to be seen wearing his hood.

I decided to follow this student to his first period class to make a point with him, hopefully ONE last time! At his classroom door, I motioned for him to come out into the hallway. The look on his face told me that he knew he had messed up because he could see by my expression that I wasn't happy. I questioned what reason he had for putting his hood back on after I had asked him to take it off? He didn't respond. I simply told him that I was through "playing this game" with him, and the next time he was seen with his hood on, he would serve a handful of days sitting in the Dean's office. He quickly acknowledged he understood…

Not long after the school day started, I found out that my efforts to allow our current EL newcomer students to stay at Apollo for next year fell short. The district **did** confirm that the students and their families could apply for a transfer, but they would have to provide their own transportation to Apollo in the mornings. The superintendent explained that board policy prohibits the extra bus routes to pick up students who have transferred. It would be different if the routes were already in place and the students had seats to occupy. I completely understand the need for the policy and why these decisions have to be made at the district level. I was hoping in the case of these students and their newcomer status that a change to policy (or exception at the very least) could be considered before next year. Again, we just want what is in the best interest for these students. The allowance for the transfer **will** help, but most of these students and their families have no means of transportation... Strike two!

Later in the day, I found out that all of my recent coaching efforts with a teacher have not paid off, and mounting evidence reveals that the same habits have continued. Despite my efforts to help, it was painfully evident that more drastic measures would be needed. For the third time today, I felt that my presence made **zero** difference... bordering on **insignificant**!

This is precisely the reason I have requested a timeline for letting individuals know first and then staff know of my retirement at the end of this year. While I have to be fair to allow the next principal enough time to establish him/herself and the staff to get acquainted, I am not at all looking forward to any more days of feeling insignificant. It is only natural that employees start looking past the "guy who will soon be retired" and start asking questions of others. In sixteen days, in our regularly scheduled faculty meeting, the entire staff will be informed of my intentions to retire, and I will also explain the timeline for hiring my replacement. Between now and March 23, I will choose times to inform members of the Leadership Team, asking each one of them to allow me the opportunity to tell everyone among the staff in my own way. I trust them completely to follow through with that request.

Trying my best to brush aside this glum feeling I have acquired at the end of this dreary Monday, I look forward to our plans for tomorrow - ACT Testing for grades 10 and 11. To achieve this, we will need every available staff member to help with proctoring and accommodating special education students. For the staff and their hard work to pull this day off, the school has acquired some money for the Real Hacienda food truck to pay for each staff member's pre-ordered meal. **THAT**, in itself, is something to look forward to!

March 9, 2022 - On this day after the ACT, we focused on getting back into our regular routine. On ENL this morning, I asked our students to finish this grading period strong and complete everything needed in their classes to get their grades in good standing. The biggest problem with making this type of announcement is the students who really need to hear them are rarely paying attention. Still, these conditions cannot be ignored with any hope that the students will correct their academic deficiency on their own!

In the past thirty-two years, the one thing that has changed the most is the conditions that exist in the homes of school-aged children. More students live in single-parent conditions today, and far more students live with adults who are not their parents (foster families or other relatives). A majority of these households provide all the care and nurturing needed for the students to be successful, but there are too many whose conditions do not. In these cases, the students do not have the support they need to focus on school or anything that would have a positive impact in getting them to a functional status in society. In **these** cases, educators have their backs against the wall, and they have to provide ***all of the support*** for the students to find their way to graduation. ***IF*** this can be achieved, these students are left to take on society from that point forward.

Today we had our third "Seniors-N-Danger" meeting of the semester between the administrators, our senior guidance counselor, our Student Success Coach, and our EL Instructional Coach (6 adults). For these meetings, the senior guidance counselor runs a failure report for 12th graders and takes the time to go through the list to weed out any senior who is failing a class that is not needed for graduation. Too often, a condition called "senioritis" kicks in, and some seniors in ***supportive*** homes give up on the work they need to complete in those classes in which credits won't keep them from graduating with a HS Diploma.

I take the list and add it to a spreadsheet (in a new tab) so that we can compare it to the previous list in search of students who have improved their status. For this report today, our efforts had reduced the list of failing seniors from eighty-four (84) three weeks ago to fifty-eight (58). Of these students, we determined that twenty-two had been on this list repeatedly and were the students we needed to focus our main efforts on via phone calls home and conferences here at school. Sadly, ten of these students were in a worse condition on today's report than they were three weeks ago, and the bulk of them were failing three or more required classes needed for graduation. Despite the efforts of four and sometimes five adults working with these students (***other than*** their teachers!), they cannot care enough to make the necessary effort to ***help themselves***! The rest of the students on the failure report (36) are either failing one class or have been making adequate progress in multiple classes, and the team feels that they will make it by the end of the year.

This is one aspect going on in education today that the public has no knowledge of – all the effort and support provided by adults just to get students to stay on track to graduate! As I mentioned in several journal entries last semester, we had issues dealing with student apathy **prior** to the pandemic. The past two years have only made this worse. Too many of our students refuse to do work **IN** class, much less work that we would have asked students to do twenty years ago as **homework**. Authentic homework does not exist in many of our classes today, at least at the HS level. Even still, some of our students cannot bring themselves to complete the work during class when the teachers allow it. For these students, school is essentially a "hangout," and their hardest task on any given day is getting up in the morning....

YES...! Conditions in education have certainly changed in the last thirty-two years! Schools like Apollo MUST work to find solutions for the student apathy and lack of direction, or it will consume them. If students cannot see the **purpose** for a high school education and use it to better **prepare for their adult life after graduation**, what **good** are the adult's efforts while the kids are in school?

March 10, 2022 (Bomb Threat!) - I had been looking forward to this day because our Engineering/Programming Instructor had invited me and three other adults to serve as the Shark Tank panel for two groups of his students who have been working on their team projects since the very beginning of the year. This computer science competition requires that the teacher leave the teams to discover and troubleshoot on their own as they build their product from the ground up. In essence, the teacher cannot teach the students!

When it comes to invitations to see our students give a presentation demonstrating a product that they have put their blood, sweat, and tears into, I jump at the chance to join them. To portray one of the "sharks" on Shark Tank, I go the distance by offering some challenging questions to heighten the experience for the students. The students did a **tremendous** job! Each group knew their product well, and each member contributed an equal amount during the presentation. By and large, the groups were not too rattled by the questioning process.

As I started my way back to my office, I received a call from the front office that they needed to see me **immediately**. The problem was that I was on the complete opposite side of our campus, and we were in the middle of our last lunch, which meant having to navigate through several people. I also didn't want to cause any sense of alarm by sprinting through the hall, so I walked at a fast pace, knowing that one of the other administrators would check in before I got there.

Upon arrival, the thought I had in mind when I received the call on the radio turned out to be true — Apollo HS had received a **bomb threat**, and we were being advised to evacuate the building! Our closest neighboring high school had just received it's second bomb threat in two days, and we were preparing for a "copycat" threat on our campus. Sure enough, it happened!

Being perfectly honest, bomb threats in schools are becoming a rarity due to the tracking systems that are in place for phone calls and electronic communications. The procedures we use today are geared towards tracking the source of the threat and checking the validity of the threat more than evacuating buildings. Especially because of the nature that most bomb threats are made, I would bet that 99.999% of all bomb threats in schools are nothing more than a hoax. In fact, there are times that within a short amount of minutes we have determined that the threat is made by someone hundreds of miles away and therefore cannot be real.

This was not the case today because the threat came through on dispatch and not directly to the school. By the time we had been called by dispatch, law enforcement was already on the way to Apollo and would be entering the building. We HAD to evacuate....

This really did not sit well with me because you do NOT want to get everyone in a heightened state of anxiety unless you absolutely have to. With the lockdown that Apollo HS experienced on August 26 of this year and the event still being pretty fresh on everyone's minds, there is no need to create any more panic!

Although it is not something that schools *practice* (like other safety drills), the administration, district law enforcement, central office support staff, and the Apollo staff sprang into action like a well-oiled machine. The students and their teachers evacuated to our football stadium that is on our same campus but a quarter-mile away. Thank goodness the sun was out and the temperature was fifty-plus degrees! If it were raining, we would have to be doing the SAME thing!!

Within minutes of the evacuation, the law enforcement on-site started their help with available staff to "sweep" the school looking for anything suspicious, while my secretary and I started communicating to Apollo families and staff to keep them informed. By this time, we had already been given a couple of names as potential suspects.

In fortunate circumstances, things can progress that quickly when it comes to bomb threats. Due to the nature of this information we received and the number of adults we had to sweep the building, we made the call to start releasing students from the football stadium back to school within forty-five minutes!

During this time, my secretary and I had sent out three messages to parents to let them know of the evacuation, that students and staff were SAFE, and that we were returning to the building. Although we did everything we could to urge them NOT to come to school to pick up their child, some of our parents still showed up at the football stadium, along with some at the front office wanting us to release their child to them. The problem? We couldn't, based on the lack of proper identification needed at the football stadium and the obvious issue of students all being a quarter mile away from the front office. While this was another aggravating situation where parents were getting in our way of doing our jobs, the number of parents who actually signed their student out after the students were back in the building was twenty-five (FAR less than what we experienced on the August 26 Lockdown)....

As this day came to a close, we felt that we had all the information we needed to press felony terroristic threatening charges on at least one individual, and our School Law Enforcement Officer was busy getting the evidence he needed. I finished the day by preparing a communication for the staff to brief them on the excellent job that they did, as well as some reminders for what to do when an evacuation must take place in the future. We withheld meeting as a Leadership Team and decided to just wait to debrief at our regular weekly meeting tomorrow morning. Although this event that forced us to evacuate our building today was nowhere near the intensity level that the lockdown created back in August, it was still a mentally exhausting day....

March 11, 2022 - As if there weren't enough tension and drama at Apollo HS the past twenty hours, we had an altercation before the school day began that led to a fight in the breakfast line in front of everyone in the Commons Area. This fight involved three individuals, and it had absolutely nothing to do with the drama that led to our bomb threat evacuation yesterday. If any student's or staff member's nerves weren't already on edge before arriving at school today, they likely are now. All three individuals were escorted in different directions by administrators or law enforcement, and the rest of the adults in the Commons tried to keep everyone else calm so that we could move on about our day...

On ENL this morning, I addressed our students with the details that led to the evacuation (so they would understand "why"), and I also made it very clear that the information we had would likely be leading to felony charges being filed immediately. At the end of my message, I re-iterated the importance of our "See Something/Hear Something=SAY Something" initiative to the closest adult. Our students have always been good about this, but it is never a bad idea to remind them.

What I didn't realize is that our SLEO had already acquired more information that was looking more like the call was prompted within our own student body and NOT a former student that we had surmised at the end of the day yesterday. However, the former student *was* connected.

Because our administrators were tied down with the before-school scuffle and the discipline with parent contacts that it required, we had about half of our leadership team absent at the time of our weekly meeting. I decided that our topics were too important to start without them (one topic being the debrief of the evacuation and return to the building), so we postponed the meeting until after lunch shifts were over. In the meantime, I went straight to our SLEO Office to see what information he had.

It turns out that the information we had yesterday was factual at least to the point that the former student admitted in a text that he made the call. He actually didn't make the call as he admitted to his girlfriend in a text, but these two individuals led law enforcement directly to the individual who *did* make the call... and he is a current student at Apollo! With just a little effort, the SLEO tracked down on the security cameras where this student was located yesterday at the time the call was made, and it showed very clearly that he made a phone call. ALL the information received on this event lined up perfectly - it was just a matter of talking to the student in question and one other to confirm so that we could close this case in less than 24 hours from the bomb threat taking place… AND press felony charges. **THIS** is the reason that bomb threats in schools are rare these days!

Feeling pretty good about the direction this case was going, I went back to my office and finished some of my work and a follow-up post-conference conversation with a teacher or two. Just prior to our lunch shifts beginning, we filed charges related to the bomb threat and escorted the instigator out of the school and into our SLEO cruiser. I cannot reinforce enough the **dynamic work** of our SLEO and the District Law Enforcement nor reiterate how rare it is to receive bomb threats in schools. With FELONY charges filed and the awareness of the student body with the individual involved, we are hoping that this puts an end to any bomb threats! Our students and staff are blessed to have our SLEO!

One item that I have had on my agenda starting this week is initiating personal conversations with individual leadership team members informing them of my plans to retire at the end of this year. Instead of having one conversation with the team this next Friday at the regular weekly meeting, I felt that I owed it to each one of the members to individually have a conversation that would include their own personal details for moving forward. By the end of this day, I have reached about half of the leadership team, and with each one, I have asked their help in keeping this news between us so that I have the opportunity to share with ALL individuals in this building. As I have mentioned before, I fully trust my leadership team in following through with this request. Twelve days and counting until all staff will be informed….

As each conversation takes place, I feel a little bit more relieved that the "process" has been shared. As I mentioned in my very first journal entry for the school year (August 11, 2021 of Book 1, *Humanity in Peril*), I have known that I would be retiring at the end of this year. There hasn't been a single day that I have questioned this decision, but I have every intention to work up until my last day. With each of these conversations with leadership team members, I explain the importance of our work between now and the end of the year to establish our Focus Areas determined by the ImpactKY survey results and the importance in setting up the next principal for a positive transition to next school year. This same message will be delivered to all staff on March 23 - we will see how this plan and the work unfolds from there....

March 15, 2022 - So marks the second day of the 4th 9-week grading period and the day that grades are due to be posted by the teachers. We are also finishing up with ACT testing (those who missed the original day) for juniors and sophomores. The afternoon temperatures are getting back to seventy-plus degrees, and the spring sports teams are starting their seasons. It's a busy time of year, but it's a pretty good feeling to walk outside and see/smell spring in the air. The problem is the work we have to take care of on the inside. If we can just hold out until April 1st and the start of Spring Break, we will be in good hands.

On the inside, we are still working on some drama that spilled over from last week— nothing at all related to the bomb threat. The culprit of this drama is **social media**, the downfall of society, as I have so eloquently described the platforms where DAILY both adults and children relentlessly bully others. In this saga we are dealing with today, one individual posted something back in the fall that was all but forgotten, until someone reposted it at the end of last week. At that point, the feeding frenzy ensued, and the individual reached a point that they did not feel safe at our school. The problem is that there is nothing school officials can do about inappropriate things that are posted outside of school time, UNLESS it causes issues or a disruption to the educational process at any point in the day.

When school officials have evidence to support that threats or harassment are occurring during the school day, we have grounds to issue discipline. What parents do not understand is why school officials can't be the "social media police" and suspend students for making threats or harassing comments on **their own time**. It just doesn't work that way! Thank goodness it doesn't - we would have a mess on our hands if our jurisdiction also included events that happened on the nights and weekends. Can you imagine?!?!

Then again, ANY time we hear that there has been a fight between two students in the community or that there is "friction" that could lead to aggressive behavior, the administrators ALWAYS do their best to head it off at the pass. At the very least, both parties are spoken with individually and asked if there are going to be any issues here at school. This is what we call the "warning shot across the bow." If any issues ARE brought to school, it could mean a harsher penalty because the students were warned. This is not a 100% foolproof preventative measure, but it has worked far more often than not....

Back to the culprit - thanks to social media, administrators' jobs are far more difficult today than they were when I started twenty years ago. The ONLY aspect that is helpful related to social media issues is the **evidence** that the harassing communication provides. For any **good** that social media is supposed to represent, in my humble opinion, it is NOT AT ALL worth the negative that comes with it. There are far too many people whose lives have been negatively impacted at the hands of social media, and they will never be the same as a result....

Making a clean break from the negative tone in this journal entry, the best part of this day was the annual "celebration" that took place. One of our "Rock Star" teachers who I have written about before is responsible for setting up our accommodations testing for students and the numerous adults around the building that it involves (some students are allowed readers, some are allowed multiple days to take each part of the exam - all based on their Individualized Education Program, or IEP). This teacher takes it upon herself to purchase enough BBQ and prepare several side dishes and desserts to feed a small army!! Yes, she does have some help from her 2nd Lieutenant and Rear Admiral, but the gesture is one that all adults who help with accommodations testing look forward to every year. This is her THANK YOU, and she would not consider accepting any monetary support from the school to pull this off. This is HER "show," her "signature" that makes her the unique individual she is. Every ounce of time she commits to this meal and all the effort that it takes from her or her helpers comes straight from the heart. This is another one of those events that takes place at Apollo HS, unlike anything I have seen in my thirty-two years of education. Just thinking about the effort and the *reason* why this teacher does this makes me smile....

March 17, 2022 - I am hoping that this monthly, off-campus District Principals Meeting that took place today is my last one. Not that I find no value in these meetings, but it is more because I have a hard time focusing on *any* discussion that involves next year planning, and there is *always* something going on back in the building that is needing my attention more....

It is uncanny that most of my topics in these journal entries lately have centered around issues that stem from social media. Uncanny, maybe, but not at all coincidence! Overnight, Apollo administrators were made aware of a social media communication that involved four students sending a very lewd, hateful, and inconsiderate message directed at an individual student in one of their classes. The message was long and used words, such as "To the retarded, morbidly-obese land whale..." and the communication progressively got worse from there.

Once again, the administration finds themselves in the middle of policing social media messaging that has taken place outside of the school day. What is most mind-boggling of all in this particular case was the sheer disregard by at least one of the students who did not think what he/she was saying was wrong AND the admittance that "[he/she had] said worse things before." Here we go again for the irresponsibility society has sustained in raising kids to understand the dangers connected with social media or communicating/posting messages in such a negative tone for other eyes to see. How many parents these days hand their children a smartphone and do nothing more than say, "Knock yourself out kid...!"?

In today's Principals Meeting, one of the Asst. Superintendents shared some data on a topic that was very related to the concerns that we have had with some issues we have seen these past two years at Apollo HS:

- 13 to 19 year olds - suicide is now the second leading cause of death.
- 1 in 7 of the same age category have contemplated suicide.
- Students going through gender identity struggle are 4 times more likely to commit suicide.

I'll ask the audience this question - how much do YOU believe that social media has had on the rise in these statistics? There is no doubt at all in **my mind** the answer, all based on my experience as a high school administrator these past twenty years! Back to all the reasons I highlighted in Book 1, *Humanity in Peril* – how much more of these issues can educators endure? How much more can society, itself, endure at the hands of social-media created negativity? Parents MUST understand **their responsibility** for the communications their children are posting through those $900 smartphones. I have witnessed FAR too many life-altering communications that have taken place on social-media accounts and email this school year alone. Society will fall if this does not change…!

Moving on to the more positive side of this day! One item shared at the Principals Meeting that represents a "glimmer of hope" was the mention of Grow Your Own programs that are popping up in districts across the state. A Grow Your Own administrator version is funding two-thirds of the cost of graduate school tuition for individuals who are educators aspiring to go into administration. Districts pay up as much as they can in order to offer as many scholarships as possible to aspiring administrators. With the help of one additional funding source, our district will be offering ten such scholarships. The future is brighter knowing that there will be more administrators available to take over as the current workforce retires.

Even better music to my ears was hearing that the district is initiating a Grow Your Own program for classified staff who wish to complete the required courses to obtain their teacher certification. With this program, a similar offering to pay for most of the tuition is made so that the candidate can take classes without the worry of the financial obligation, and they may be able to take more than one class at a time.

This is **great** news because there are some instructional aides and other classified individuals in schools who do ***phenomena****l* work each day and would make tremendous teachers because of their connectability with students coupled with their work ethic. Too many times in the past, financial hardship has been a barrier too hard to overcome for these individuals to even get started. Now, the scholarships remove the financial strain and allow these candidates to have a better chance at completing their program and earning their teaching degree. The timing for this couldn't be better!

March 18, 2022 - This day started with the usual Leadership Team Meeting and our discussions regarding the recent Cognia Accreditation Review Report, the staffing additions needed to be made for the 2023 year, and the non-renewal of staff by the end of this year. With good fortune, we should be able to get two postings next week that will represent the start of what we need for next year. Unfortunately, one of those two postings is the result of one of our very talented intern teachers who has accepted a job with another school nearby. While we feel this may have been inevitable due to the connections that this teacher has with this school system, we hope that there is nothing about this school year or Apollo HS that has turned her away. There was nothing negative that she indicated when she and I spoke, but it still makes me wonder. Bottom line - she has the potential to be a tremendous teacher, and we hate to lose her!

Having spoken to everyone in the Leadership Team by now regarding my retirement, it changes the stakes and the level of importance in our discussions for staffing, **especially** concerning which departments in our building would benefit from an added teacher. We always use data and current course requests for the next school year to inform these decisions, but it doesn't always mean everyone is in agreement. The Leadership Team, at least, has indicated their agreement for the two **added** positions that I will be recommending to the SBDM next week at our special meeting. Going one step further, I sent an email to all Lead Teachers (heads of each department) explaining my recommendations as well. I made the offer to have a meeting if the information I shared prompted a lot of questions. So far, as of the end of this day, I have not heard from anyone.

While in our meeting this morning, the Cafeteria Manager sent me an email asking if I could "be a Lunch Lady" today. I jumped at the opportunity, as I will **any time** I am asked from now until the end of the year. Once again, my presence prompted the questions from some of the students, such as, "Where have you been, Mr. Lasley?!" Of course,

I took the opportunity to spin a little yarn and tell the students that the ladies had fired me but decided to give me another chance. This brought chuckles and grins that made my heart feel good to see! The interactions and the connections made in this ninety-minute time period were just what I needed after a long week filled with more than average drama.

Another positive moment that we were able to fit in on this day was a conversation between one of the assistant principals, our math student teacher who was spending her last day with us, and me. In this meeting, we explained that she would be seeing a math posting early next week and that we encouraged her to apply. This student teacher mentioned that she thoroughly enjoyed her student teaching experience here at Apollo, she praised her mentor teacher and let us know how good she was to her, and she finished by saying that she loved Apollo and would love the opportunity to join the staff next year! While promises cannot be given when these conversations take place, it at least gives the candidates as well as the school a feeling that there is hope to make something happen!

As I was winding down at the end of this day, lost in my thoughts and starting my journal entry, one of our "Rock Star" lead teachers stopped by to put something in the office vault. We engaged in a little side-bar conversation about some construction issues that keep popping up in her room. While we were talking, she asked if I were considering retirement, having heard from the superintendent that there are three principal hires needed before the start of next school year. Although she was not given my name as one of them, she had a hunch that it may be.

I told her that "it had been on my mind," but I had not made any deci- sions yet. I had to fib a little just to throw her off until next Wednesday at our faculty meeting. In our conversation, she mentioned how much she has appreciated my work and dedication in getting us through these troubled times and that I have done a good job. Being perfectly honest, this comment and conversation has been rare, for me at least. This is one thing that I have found to be true (maybe it is different for other principals - I can only speak for myself!). Employees do NOT praise the boss! Whether they feel it is true or not, nobody wants to be "*that* person." As far as my superiors over the course of twenty years as an administrator… I can recall mentions of the outstanding job my staff and I did when we were working through the lockdown last semester or other special events that required our immediate attention, but nothing comes to mind as far as just the mention of "you're doing a good job." For anyone who may need personal praise as a motivator to keep moving through the trenches of administration, you may want to think again. While this has never been important to me, it is still something very hard not to notice….

March 22, 2022 (SBDM Notified) - I took an intentional "pass" on a journal entry for yesterday. The one event that really set the tone for the day was far too painful to mention. More details may be mentioned between now and the end of the school year, but I will at least pass on all the love, prayers and support to one of Apollo's finest for their continued medical journey….

Today we had nine visitors join us from a school in Bowling Green to get our input on the "modified block" schedule that we have used at Apollo for four out of the last five years (we used a 4x4 block to get us through the pandemic last year to support predominantly virtual learning). This school has been contemplating a change in their seven-period day schedule for two years now, and their faculty cannot land on the schedule they can all agree on. Our lead guidance counselor did a good job in setting up this morning's visit and lined up all the necessary stakeholders to give multiple perspectives, offering "the good, the bad, and the ugly" of our Modified Block Schedule.

As I offered my twenty-year administrator experience with scheduling, I explained that there is no such thing as a "perfect" schedule and that pros/cons need to be considered based on the **students'** best interests before moving forward. Too many of Apollo's teachers have given up on the **student** benefits of our schedule based on the difficulties the schedule has created for **them** professionally. While these difficulties are genuine, it comes down to the school making the decision on a schedule that best supports the **students and the programs** that are offered at the school. It's not at all an easy task, and it is certain to evolve over time based on everchanging student and program needs....

I also observed one of our six intern teachers at Apollo HS this morning to represent her Cycle 3 observation. Like many first-year teachers, this intern has some growth opportunities to work on (but, in all honesty, much better than I was **my** intern year!). The most refreshing aspect of this teacher (like most of our intern experiences these past two years!) is her ability to connect with students and quickly gain their respect and attention. Her math knowledge and skills are not at all perfect, but content is truly **secondary** to the relationship-building and ability to nurture students to meet their needs daily. Content and teaching strategies can easily be taught and learned by adults over time. The ability to form relationships or be a "people person" **cannot**. Bottom line, this particular intern represents another "glimmer of hope" for the future of education.

Today marked the day in the timeline that I had previously proposed to the superintendent that I would inform the Apollo SBDM of my inten- tions to retire. As the meeting unfolded, and we covered all the items that were detailed in the agenda, we reached the "Other" category agenda item that is typically left for someone on the council or a visitor to ask questions or make comments. This time, the "other" item was mine alone.

Before explaining to the council my intentions, I asked any non-members if they would leave (considering the meeting was concluded). The student representative (representing the Apollo Student Council) who has been faithful to the SBDM all year, I allowed to stay. I asked every member to give me twenty-four hours so I could have the opportunity to explain to the faculty, myself, that I would be retiring at the end of the year. While I stumbled out of the gate in my explanation, I was very comfortable and confident in what I shared with them. My time at Apollo is coming to a close. My "tank" is empty based on the exhausting work over the past two pandemic years. I am ready to move on to my book projects....

I explained to the council the timeline for the naming of the next principal after the school year is complete. With this timeline, we can finish our busy end to the year without the worry of distractions and extra work with interviews and announcements. The SBDM Council seemed to understand what I shared with them, and they appreciated the heads up. I am hoping my communication with the faculty tomorrow will go just as easy....

March 23, 2022 (Gorilla off my back...) - I will say I was a little nervous in the hours leading up to the faculty meeting, not because I had any question about my decision or concern for becoming emotional but because I just didn't want to stumble on my words. In times like this, I find that it is helpful to start off with a funny story. While those who know me would concur that I would **never** make it as a stand-up comedian, this story was true, and it happened to me about a month ago....

Everyone has those close friends who are older. When you pass a certain age, you make a point to remind those who are close to you that **they** are older. It doesn't matter if they are one day older or nine months older, you have something on them that they cannot take away or deny: **THEY** are **OLDER.**

My older friend and I were hanging out at an establishment, and I ran into a former student of mine from my second year of teaching! Because of the path that I followed after my start in education, it has easily been twenty-five years since I had last seen this student. We ex- changed the usual, "Good to see you! How have you been?" and then went on about our own business with the company we each arrived with. It wasn't long when this former student was having a conversa- tion with the owner and mentioned how long it had been since she had seen Mr. Lasley and how neat it was to see me hanging out with my **son**…(?) TRUE STORY! As you can imagine, the owner and my close friend had a blast with this, and they continue to do so to this day!

With a lead-in like this, how can you not chuckle a little or at least smile? As the chuckles faded, the tone in the Media Center was a little somber as I segued into my announcement of retirement at the end of the year. I explained that I have been carrying this secret for some time and that I am prepared for what lies ahead. While I had their attention, I also explained how what started out as a means to relieve some stress or "vent" through writing journal entries was quickly transitioning into Book 1, *Humanity in Peril*, and it would be available at least in eBook format by the end of the school year. I explained to the teachers that my time at Apollo HS has been the most rewarding of my career, even while the past two years have brought the most challenge. I finished by telling them that we still had some work to do in completing this year and that I would do my best to set the next principal up for success moving forward. Within ten minutes, I had delivered my news, and I left the faculty in the Media

Center so they could have some privacy while they voted for SBDM teacher member for the next cycle.

On my way home, I felt a peace that I had not felt in a *long* time, as if a gorilla had just climbed off my back. Before I arrived at home, I made a special stop to spend some time with my "son" and share the news with him....

March 24, 2022 (the Day After...) - This day started out on a positive note as several teachers and staff members made a point to stop and tell me congratulations while I was making my way around the building. It meant a lot to hear their words and support as we also discussed the progress on my book (*Humanity in Peril*). While a few of them mentioned that they were sad to see me go, they were happy for me and my family, and they wished me the best.

Today marked a special day for me, as I also completed my very last *formal* observation with our ASL Teacher. I am so proud of the progress she has made this year and her embrace of the ATIP process and feedback given by the committee members. This teacher is another "glimmer of hope" in the next generation of teachers, as Apollo HS represents a pioneer in the teaching of ASL as a foreign language credit. With hope, along with the **continued requests** made by students to take ASL 1 and ASL 2 courses, this course offering will not only catch on in our building, but also across the state. There is so much GOOD that can come from this, and it will take Apollo's example to foster ASL programs in other high schools.

As an added bonus today, I had made plans to help cashier and be a "lunch lady." I mentioned to the cafeteria manager earlier this week that I wanted to help them once per week (at least) between now and the end of the year, so I could increase my capacity to connect with the students before I retire. THIS is the part that I will miss the most, not that it has to be as a cashier, but anything that puts me in close contact with the students. To say "thank you" and call each student by name as they walk by and hear a "thank you" or "have a good day" in return makes me light up inside and out. Admittedly, I do know quite a few student names, but I see their name on the monitor when they scan their code in. Either way, it is a method I have used all year to make a personal connection with each student, and I have noticed it makes a tremendous difference! Many of these students are quicker to acknowledge me throughout the building or tell me "hi" before I have the chance to. **RELATIONSHIPS** have been a centerpiece of my existence as an educator for thirty-two years, and I firmly believe that it will always represent the key to reaching, teaching, and motivating students!

The icing on the cake moment that *made* this day very special was finding out that my bueno amigo "Pascual" had earned Student-of-the-Month for his grade level. "Pascual" is one of my EL friends who comes through the Global Fare line frequently, along with his other EL friends, and he is also one that I have been fighting to be allowed to continue as an Apollo HS student next year, even though he will be leaving the newcomer program after this year. Although he lives on the opposite side of the county, his family is thrilled with his progress here at Apollo this year, and they want very much for him to stay. "Pascual" has come a long way since the beginning of this year, and the fact that his teachers would nominate him and vote for him to represent his class of 370 students is a testament to his work. "Pascual" *earned* this recognition, and he has made a home here at Apollo HS. The fact that we have the support system in place for students like "Pascual" to thrive is a perfect reason that he should be allowed to stay. Again, **NOBODY** loves our kids as much as we do….

March 29, 2022 - I submitted my Intent to Retire form yesterday, and I must say that it felt a little weird in doing so. Although I have not wavered on my decision since the beginning of this school year, *saying* that you are retiring and *taking action to start the process* are like two repelling forces! This morning, the Apollo HS Principal position was posted. This pretty much makes it official at this point. From this point forward, every action and every conversation I have will be *different* and will take on a feeling that will be hard for me. I am not used to working and applying effort towards an end product that I know I will not be a part of. This may be hard for others to understand. In thirty-two years, I have never worked up until the end of a school year **KNOWING** that I was going to be doing something else after the year ended. Any time I made a transition to another school or from teaching to administration, it has always happened during the summer....

As this day unfolded, I started making my way around the building talking to some of the teachers I am responsible for evaluating and walking them through the Summative Evaluation process. Because most of our work was completed for what is considered the "full" evaluation (with documents attached as evidence), this process is more of a formality for any teacher, UNLESS they are not getting the work done and are in danger of not having their contract renewed. For my caseload of teachers on their summative cycle, this concern is not even remotely a topic of conversation. I have been there before, but thankfully, only a handful of times in my career. Although it is not an enjoyable conversation to take part in, it just comes with the job as a principal.

Today we sponsored our annual College Fair for juniors, filling the small gym with forty-two different college representatives. Not only was it amazing to see this many guests in a relatively small space, it was incredible to see our students being able to visit each table and pick up information or trinkets from these colleges or universities. Keep in mind this is the **very first opportunity** we have had for this type of event in over two years! While a good handful of our students likely did not make the connection that they are the first junior class to have the opportunity, I can tell you the adults who were witness to the event all had smiles on their faces. The common conversation between myself and a few other Apollo adults centered around how good it felt to see this event happen and how "normal" it made us feel.

The College & Career Readiness team **ALWAYS** does a phenomenal job in making these events happen. Kudos to them for their dedication to our students!

I also had the last cycle meeting for one of our ATIP teachers, as we are starting to wrap up the summative process for each of them. This particular intern has done an incredible job embracing the ATIP experience and focusing on the growth items the committee has shared with her. She has plenty of evidence of growth over the course of the year, and the committee of four math educators unanimously agreed that she has been a tremendous supporter of her PLC (professional learning community). Once again, this intern represents another "glimmer of hope" for the future of education, and I am thrilled to have been a small part of her initiation into teaching.

One of the last tasks I had for the day was meeting with our administration and senior guidance counselor to get an update on our seniors failing required classes needed for graduation. These meetings (dubbed "Seniors-N-Danger") include administrators or other senior-connected adults in the building working together to get certain seniors to FOCUS enough to earn the credits they need to graduate. This meeting today represented our fifth scheduled meeting since the start of the semester in January.

After looking at the failure report, we determined that nine seniors, who have repeatedly made the list and have made little progress, should reach the status of **GRAVE** danger of not graduating. For these nine seniors, we decided that it was time to call the parents or guardians and explain that their son or daughter would soon be taken off the list for participating in the graduation ceremony and that their best chance of receiving a diploma would be attending summer school and making up the necessary credits. Once again, it boggles my mind that it has taken the efforts of five or six adults consistently making contact with these students and their parents, and they *still* are not expending the effort to *earn* the diploma that will have *their* name written on it. A majority of these nine seniors will *finally* make it once they realize we haven't been bluffing in our conferences with them, but it is sad it takes this level of effort to get them to finish.

The *good* part of this meeting has been the number of success stories that we acknowledged and highlighted on the list. These are students who have gone from failing multiple classes at the end of January to one or none before Spring Break. Most of these success stories are due to the intentional efforts of the "Seniors-N-Danger" process, but there is no way that we could have gone from fifty students on this list to less than twenty without the help of our Student Success Coach (SSC). His sole purpose is to meet with students daily and weekly in an effort to keep them in school consistently AND keep them motivated and focused on their education. He was officially hired around Thanksgiving but did not start until the first week of December 2021. He has made a world of difference with these students (at *all* grade levels!), and I can say that the list of nine seniors would be much longer if he weren't around to make his presence known. I am looking forward to seeing the progress we make on this list after Spring Break...

March 31, 2022 - Nothing compares to the love and support for each other that I have witnessed at Apollo HS. There is nothing more important than attending to your own health and the health/needs of close family members. In the past four years, Apollo HS has had more than its share of adults who have battled health conditions that have kept them away from school for long periods of time. When this involves serious health concerns from members of your own faculty/staff, it is typical that there is a rally of support and prayers for those who are affected. At Apollo HS, it sure seems the Eagle Family takes it a step further....

Just recently, information has been shared by two teachers about health concerns that will take them away from their work for an extended period of time. One of these teachers is spending her last day of the school year tomorrow, taking early maternity leave to care for the health of her unborn child. Upon delivery of her child, he will need immediate attention that will require the family to move near the hos- pital that will be able to give the best care. This teacher is one I would consider "Rock Star" status for her level of dedication to standards, attention to teaching strategies, and hard work and emerging leader- ship ability; however, saying that this school year has been a challenge for her is putting it mildly... and very little of the challenges she has experienced stem from anything she could control.

For this teacher, I have done my best to support her every step of the way as each challenge was unveiled. It is hard to accept that this will be the last time that I experience working with her, not to mention the uncertainty for her continued work as an educator moving forward. As I finish my career and move forward in my retirement, my thoughts and prayers will be with her and her family as they continue to meet each challenge head-on. This is one of many updates in which I will be expecting the Eagle Family to keep me informed....

Back to the positive side of conditions at Apollo HS. The "glimmer of hope" realization at this point in the semester (compared to last) is the **overall** improvement in the behavior of our students. While we still have our challenges from time to time (like the poor decisions made by the student who initiated the bomb threat), the weekly occurence of fights and extreme behavior among ninth graders from this past semester has significantly subsided.

This change has not happened overnight, nor has it happened on its own. This correction has been due to the efforts of the adults in the building not only disciplining those who go too far, but also in establishing more personal relationships with students at the same time. Between the administration, the teachers, the counselors, and other support staff (like our SSC), there is very intentional work in making daily connections with students in an effort to make the students feel at home. For some of these students, this is the only positive adult in- fluence that they experience, and some of the adults represent father/ mother-figures that they desperately need. These connections are, for me, the very best part of the experience as an educator, and they have been the cornerstone of my philosophy as a teacher and administrator. I found out very early on in my career that the relationships you establish with students are critical to their success in school. The old adage, "Students won't care what you know until they know that you care" is profoundly true in many cases! The more the adults in schools make the students feel at ease, respected as individuals, safe, and valued as learners, the more they will be invested in the work that is asked of them. For some of these students, depending on the amount of trauma they have experienced growing up, it takes more adults and more effort to get them to a point where they can function in schools and have any chance at success later on. EVERY effort made by adults for this purpose, whether successful or not, is well worth it…!

April 1, 2022 (So PROUD of our kids!) - I took this last day before Spring Break off because one of our children needed some help. This is one of those times that you drop what you are doing and give attention to your family….

If you believe in karma, you might say that it has paid me a visit more than once in my life. As I have explained in Book 1, my wife Angela and I are blessed to have four children. Three of our children are old enough to be on their own, contributing to society in their own way. Our oldest son, Todd, has been pretty independent since his first year in college and would be the least frequent of our children to visit home. The irony is he **lived the closest**, only seventy-five minutes from home. Because of the sarcastic world within which I plant myself on occasion, I would always describe Todd to others as, "the child who might as well live in Alaska" ….

Today I drove Todd to Carbondale, Illinois to catch a train that would start his journey in his move to Seattle, Washington. Since the pandemic began in our area two years ago, Todd has been isolated in his apartment working from home as a software engineer at a company in Louisville, Kentucky (work he initially found gratifying). Since the pandemic began, however, the team members he had enjoyed working with started finding other jobs, eliminating the "luster" that the work once possessed. If you can imagine working *and* living within the same small space for two years at a time when very few people ventured out as a means of gathering or entertainment, it is depressing to say the very least. As hard as it may be to see one of your children move a great distance from home, the desire for them to be happy quickly takes precedence....

As I drove Todd to his destination today, it brought me back to the drive that we had nearly ten years ago, when we moved Todd into his dorm. For those who have not experienced your first child moving off to college, it is an emotional roller-coaster. In that ride to deliver him to the beginning of his future, I can remember trying to get in a lifetime of conversations during the ninety-minutes we had, making sure Todd knew what to do in a variety of situations. This conversation today was different, as we took advantage of the time to just catch up on the latest with extended family and our favorite college sports team news.

Once again, Angela and I are truly blessed to have the children that we have. We are so proud of each of them and the paths they have taken. As parents, it doesn't really matter **what** your children choose to do in life, but that they treat **every** person they meet with respect and that they contribute positively to society, as well as the communities they live in... AND that they are happy!

We wish Todd the very best as he sets off on a brand-new journey. May he always be true to himself and find peace along the way....

April 11, 2022 (Bluetooth Earbuds...!) - The first day back after a break is always tough. Your sleeping patterns are all messed up, and you walk in near your normal arrival time at school feeling a little like a zombie. What made this first day back from spring break even tougher was the medical emergency that we had well before the school day began.

We had a male student report to the guidance office complaining of chest pains. The young man was visibly shaking and had recently been to the ER with similar issues and the same feelings that came over him on the bus ride to school this morning. The adults, between the nurses station, the guidance office, and the main office, all did a wonderful job as one group made contact with a parent while the other groups provided immediate care for the student and called 9-1-1. It seemed a very short amount of time before the ambulance and first responders arrived. In a matter of twenty minutes from the original call, the student was in the back of an ambulance and on his way to meet his father at the hospital. Nothing like a medical emergency to snap you back to reality in the early morning minutes after spring break! Thankfully, the student was responding well to the care given by the EMTs and had a very short drive to get to the hospital….

After the school day began, I spent the biggest part of my morning moving around the building checking in on individuals who needed a little support based on personal issues they were having and also greeting staff, welcoming them back and asking if they enjoyed their break. For many of these conversations, those of us who stayed home agreed that the weather over the entire week was one of the worst we had seen! Despite this lament, we quickly commented that the Sunday weather was wonderful, and it was good to have time off from work. It is always good to make these connections the morning after a break to see as many people as you can and to also hear the exploits of those who actually had the opportunity to travel. It is good for the soul on the day back to be able to recount some of the good times that were had!

The "back to reality" moment that I experienced today was in finding out that one of our "Dynamo" instructional coaches had accepted a district level position that she was well-suited for. This was no surprise to me, knowing that she has made the impact she has in her role within the walls at Apollo. It has likewise been apparent that the district has been impressed with her work as well. This is the nature of the work that you put in as an administrator, nurturing the up-and-coming leaders in your building. The good ones never last very long, as they are quickly considered for advanced opportunities. I know that the Apollo staff will be happy for her in taking on this new opportunity, but I also know that she will be sorely missed at the same time. I selfishly find myself being thankful that I will NOT be around next fall to experience it....

I also found out today that we have another teacher who has elected to retire at the end of this year. This makes three teachers retiring, two classified staff, and myself for a total of six at Apollo HS... for now. I am hoping that we do not find out any more, but I understand that may change in the next few weeks. With three other teachers (including the instructional coach) leaving Apollo for other opportunities, there will be several positions to hire for and plenty of change to start the next year!

One of the most frustrating aspects of this day was when the aforementioned "Dynamo" and I spoke to one of our ninth-grade female students who was not doing well in two of her core classes. We had spoken to her mother (who understood very little English) just before the break, sharing our concerns and mentioning the likelihood that her daughter would need to attend summer school. Mother understood and agreed that summer school was a necessary step if her daughter failed any of her classes.

Today, we had our first opportunity to speak with the student, after having had conversations with the teachers in her core classes. Just as her teachers mentioned, this student agreed that she was very capable to do the work the teachers asked of her in class; she just elected not to (or had a hard time initiating her work). She agreed that nobody was distracting her in her classes and that summer school didn't seem like much fun. She left my office having accepted the fact that she needed to put forth a lot more effort in her classes these last twenty-seven days of the school year... or *part* of her summer would be spent coming back to school!

As this student turned to leave my office, I caught a glimpse of her bluetooth earbuds she was wearing that were easily hidden from her long black hair! The issue is not that she is completely distracted by them, as she obviously carried on a conversation with us. The issue is that she LIKELY will take time in her classes listening to music *instead* of what the teachers are saying! This is yet another epidemic distraction that our students are immersed in today and an incredible challenge for our teachers. It is hard enough to walk around our building in the mornings or between classes greeting students, and a good portion of them blankly stare past you (wearing earbuds) as if you said nothing at all. It is still harder to accept the fact that many of our students try to leave them in while sitting in class! I have observed some of our students being very sneaky about keeping one earbud in (on the side opposite their teacher), even though our teachers for the most part do a good job making our students take them out. FRUSTRATING doesn't begin to describe the challenge that this puts on our teachers. The most disappointing aspect for me is that our *society* has allowed this to happen....

One of the last things I did before leaving today was to be certain that our teachers of this student knew to look out for her earbuds....

April 13, 2022 - For a second day this week, we had a 9-1-1 emergency with a student. This time, the student had a seizure in the middle of one of our block periods. The positive part of this event was that the teachers who were in the room saw that something wasn't right with the student and were by his side to help ease him to the floor. The bad part is that this student had no history of seizures, which puts us on a higher alert status as we work through the details and communications between the front office, nurse's station, and the dispatch operator.

The new building that we moved into at the start of this semester features an emergency call button in every classroom. This was the first time that we had an opportunity to test it for **real** (students have pressed the button on several occasions, not realizing the purpose). Between this call button, the communications between the nurse's station, the response of the administration/SLEO, and the care that the teachers gave the student, this event was handled as professionally as it could have.

Not only did the teachers do a wonderful job, the students who were in the classroom also handled it well at the same time. Normally, we would empty the classroom and send the students to another location until the seizing student was removed and in the care of the EMT staff. The problem…? This student went down at the doorway of the classroom.

As I arrived with the school nurse to help at the scene, the students were dead-silent and focusing their attention on the work they had been assigned and away from the student on the floor receiving care. This classroom, thankfully, was a co-teaching classroom where the "regular" teacher and special education teacher are responsible as a **team** to deliver instruction and serve the needs of all students. In this case, one teacher was taking care of the class while the other was providing care to the student at the doorway. BOTH of these teachers are true "Rock Stars" in my book (for the work that they do on a **daily** basis), and the AMAZING job they did today…!

Because I very much needed some positivity from the excitement this week, I offered my help today as a cashier at "my" Global Fare Line. It was a good break from the work I had been involved with earlier in the day as well as the excitement from the emergency, and I was able to make the connections I needed to get my spirits in the right place. What a difference spending time with students can make!

One of my last responsibilities for the day was communicating one final plea to get our EL newcomer students to spend at least one more year at Apollo. The communication that I sent the Central Office staff in February did at least provide the families with the option to request a transfer from the school the students are **supposed** to attend next year and **stay** at Apollo. The only problem is that transportation was not agreed to be provided, and most of these families have no means to deliver their children to school.

In this final plea, I used the example of "Pascual" who had been awarded Student of the Month for March and the fact that he was well thought of by his teachers for the progress he has made in their class. His mother is very proud of him as well and wants him to continue at Apollo so that he can experience more success after having established a home and making connections with the adults who work with him. "Pascual" is just one example, and there are a handful of others who deserve to stay in the environment where they can experience the most success. The smiles on the faces of these students is all I need to know and understand to continue to advocate for them… No translation necessary!

Within a short amount of minutes, the superintendent replied to all of the recipients that I included in my communication to say, "Rick, we will devote the time and effort to fully consider what you have outlined in your email in our next leadership team meeting. I know you are advocating for what you feel is in the total best interest of these students and their families." This is all I can ask - my hope is that they consider what is honestly best for the students in question. Time will tell….

April 15, 2022 (It is time…) - This was a special day for me from beginning to end. To start, my original plans to travel to Frankfort, Kentucky to meet at the KASA Office were averted by a last-minute decision to meet virtually. This meant that I could save four hours of travel time, miles on the truck, and I would be able to get back to Apollo much sooner than expected and actually get some work done! To top this off, I was able to take my time getting up and enjoy some coffee before the meeting started.

Once I arrived at work, I realized that it was past time for me to communicate my intentions to retire to the staff at Apollo HS, as well as the families who send their kids to our school. For the staff, it is complicated due to the vast number of individuals who serve Apollo in a variety of capacities with a variety of work schedules, some not working during the actual school day. Although I would have wanted to speak with them in person (as I did with the faculty), the best I would be able to do for the staff was to send an email.

For the families of Apollo, I wanted to make them aware that the Principal Selection Process would be starting next week, and they would be given details of the timeline for that process (training, interviews, decision, announcement). Just to be clear, I wanted it to be well-known to our families for the conditions of my departure. In this day and time with social media, it would not take much for someone to start a rumor that I had been **fired**! SADLY, even **with** my communication I made today, the chance of rumors starting is always possible….

With the staff communication, I made it very clear how blessed I have been to spend the time I have had working with the dedicated individuals within the Eagle Family. Despite the conditions that we have worked under these past two years, the time I have spent at Apollo HS has been the most rewarding for a variety of reasons. This says a lot due to the rewarding experiences I have had working in two districts before Daviess Co. As I mentioned in Book 1, *Humanity in Peril*, I have been blessed to work alongside many colleagues whom I have carried with me over the years (see the November 23, 2021 - Thanksgiving Edition journal entry), and I owe them all **gratitude** for helping shape **ME** into the person that I am today.

Typically, it is hard not to be emotional when it comes to making these types of communications, especially when it is leading to the end of your career! For me, I have not wavered for a second since the very beginning of this school year (August 11, 2021) when I informed my wife, Angela, of my intentions. I have witnessed many before me who have battled with making the decision to retire, some regretting their decision after the fact. I am fortunate in that regard, I guess. Knowing that I have a plan to fulfill the conclusion of these books I have written and to (in **ANY** capacity) continue supporting public education certainly helps. Being completely committed and ready for what is next for a retiree **truly** is key....

Before this day ended, there were a handful of staff members who had read my email and made the choice to respond and thank me for what I have done to help them. THOSE messages are the ones that mean so much and stay with you for a lifetime. As I mentioned in a prior journal entry, principals rarely and seldom are thanked for their work, commitment, and dedication. It DOES happen, but it puts far too many employees in an awkward position to communicate praise to the "boss." I completely understand and can certainly take this into consideration as I appreciate any genuine messages that are sent my way between now and the end of this year....

Although I missed the Easter Egg Hunt (eggs filled with candy and some donated money for students to find as they walk the halls between classes) put on by our student council, it truly was an awesome way to complete a **long** week returning from Spring Break!

April 18, 2022 (Ode to the Cafeteria Lady…!) - I can remember my first year at Apollo HS learning my way around the building and trying to remember names. I was quickly amazed by the work ethic and camaraderie displayed by our cafeteria staff. These ladies were very dedicated to please the students and staff, and they had just received an award that named them "Cafeteria Staff of the Year" for their hard work and commitment. Less than half of the ladies who worked in our cafeteria six years ago are still here, but the same level of dedication to our students and staff is demonstrated on a daily basis.

Some schools have cafeteria staff who do not feel a part of the rest of the staff. Some schools' cafeteria staff rarely come out of the kitchen to be seen by anyone else. Some schools do not recognize their cafeteria staff as often as they should or make them a part of the regular school celebrations. At Apollo HS, these ladies are woven into the fabric that makes the Eagle Family "Tapestry" as vibrant as it is displayed each and every day.

Don't take my word for this – any visitor stopping by Apollo HS near lunch time will witness the following:

- SMILES and greetings by the cafeteria staff with the same returned
- Dancing and making connections with the students
- School Spirit and the cafeteria staff dressed for the occasion
- HUGS between cafeteria staff and students or cafeteria staff and Apollo adults
- Allowance for adults to mix up their lunch choices with items from multiple lines
- Allowance for returns or trades for students who try something and don't like it
- Indications that "We love our job!" from every cafeteria staff member without having to say it

These ladies ARE very much a part of the culture that makes **every** school like Apollo HS unique. They are vastly underpaid for what they bring to our school, and they keep coming back EVERY day with the same smiles on their faces. There are countless times I have witnessed one of the ladies attend to the needs of a student or staff member or respond to something someone has asked for, turning around and making it their mission. I honestly believe that some of these ladies would crawl through a minefield to get something for us – I can attest that they sure leave you with this impression! The Apollo HS Cafeteria Staff are an extraordinarily special bunch, and I am **darn proud** to have worked alongside them this year!

April 19, 2022 - As a HS principal especially, and maybe in some degree at the other grade levels, there are "forces" working against you from the moment that you step on campus to assume your role for the first time. Some of these forces are nearby, some far away, but they are certainly present. In some instances, the principal may be able to hold those forces at bay and get whatever work is needed to be done throughout the year. In very rare cases, the forces go away over time. Worst-case scenario, the forces are just too great to overcome, and despite what efforts are given by the principal, eventually the forces consume the principal and his/her work.

In my experience as an administrator of twenty years, I have found that the best approach in dealing with "forces" is NOT addressing them **directly**. If I, as principal, do the work that is needed for the school and what is in the best interests of the students and staff, including various input among leaders along the way, the forces **should** be contained and very manageable as a by-product....

I can just imagine what some... most... or maybe ALL readers are thinking at this point. **What in the world is he talking about??** All I can reveal at this point is to say that I have done everything in my power to avoid the "forces" at the end of my career from the time that I have started planning the timeline in my mind for my last few weeks as principal. These next four weeks will be very revealing as to whether I can have a SWEET, BITTER-SWEET, or just BITTER end to my career. Time will certainly tell....

Regardless of which three scenarios come true for me, I will continue holding firm on my stance to provide what is in the best interest of Apollo HS with every decision I make. This means, I am absolutely consulting the Leadership Team to see what their opinion is for every big decision, especially if it involves personnel, policy, or anything that is exclusive to July 1, 2022 and beyond.

Case in point– at the SBDM Meeting today, I had planned for the SBDM members to see the newly revised Discipline Code that one of the assistant principals and a committee spent four meetings revising (pretty much an "overhaul"). The reason for this work is due to the responses in our recent ImpactKY survey that indicated teachers

were not happy with the way misbehavior has been demonstrated in our students this year, AND especially, the mounting inconsistencies between the adults in this building in ***enforcing*** the expectations. I decided the work that was necessary to correct this needed OUR attention right away, and it could not wait until the next principal assumed her/his role to start the next school year. In my humble opinion, the success or failure of ANY discipline code lies predominantly in the hands of the teachers and those most responsible with discipline on a day-to-day basis... ***not*** the principal. Other educators/administrators are welcome to disagree.

For the SBDM Meeting today, it would have taken a "miracle" for the members to all look over the discipline code and unanimously agree, "Hey, this looks great!" As I mentioned to the council members today, **THE** most controversial aspect of any school's student handbook **IS** the Dress Code (every discipline code has one). Because this aspect of the revised discipline code started fielding a lot of questions and concerns for it being too "subjective," I knew that our discussion or any decision on it would be pointless. Simply put, I was not on the committee that worked on discipline code revisions, and I would not be here next year to help enforce it.

Staying true to my word, I asked that this agenda item be tabled and the conversation be picked back up at the point that the next principal was announced ***and*** prepared to work on it....

I cannot help but have just a little anxiety wondering just how much the "forces" will affect how my career ends....

April 22, 2022 - I cannot help but note the passage of time here lately. My concerns for how much things change at the point that your retirement is made public and "official" has been on target. I feel surrounded by a palpable air of silence... and it is DEAFENING!

At the end of last week, I sent my message of retirement to the Apollo families in the Weekly Newsletter. This week, there were two articles written regarding my retirement, one in the more recent digital newspaper here in Owensboro and the other in the long-standing print newspaper. Both gave similar reflections of my prior experience and also things that have changed about education over my career. **THIS** is what made my retirement very real to me, especially to hear from individuals I have worked with over the years who read the articles. My days are numbered, and it is a hard thing to prepare for, especially when the conversations are already moving past me....

Again, there is really nothing that can prepare you for this moment. Although I had asked the superintendent for the ability to finish out the year without the new principal interviews and announcement getting in the way of our work, it was determined by the SBDM Council and/ or the superintendent that the end of the school year was too long to wait. Despite my request, I have to accept that I have no control over this, and I may as well be prepared to "pass the torch" sooner rather than later. It's just hard to relinquish "control" when you have been the primary decision maker of a school for over seventeen years....

The comfort that keeps me going is the occasional and random student who may stop me in the hall to tell me that they read the paper about my retirement and how I had been a "great principal" for their time at Apollo. Other staff members within Apollo HS, as well as district staff who frequent Apollo HS, have mentioned that they are sad to hear of my retirement, but they wish me the best. While these comments are certainly gratifying, I need to stay grounded and use them to help me focus on my day-to-day work and keep putting one foot in front of the other. These next four weeks could be the hardest I have ever had in my career; then again, they may be the most gratifying. I simply do not know....

My daughter, Lauren, reached out to the family this week to let us know that she had successfully passed her student-teaching experience. This was based on her last observation and conference with her university professor and current mentor teacher. We are all excited, happy, and UBER-PROUD of Lauren! Talk about surreal!! Adding to this good news, she has been contacted for an interview in the Shelby County Schools system this next week for an Elementary Music position. I have advised her to be sure to "do her homework" about the school prior to the interview and to find out if the district is considered to be "arts-friendly." As a very stable back-up plan, Lauren has also taken the High School Math Praxis exam and passed it with flying colors... Yes, she gets that after her dad...!

I also had the pleasure of speaking with Apollo's Bowling Coach while watching Apollo Softball take on our district rival. I had awarded her son the Apollo Principal Leadership Award two years ago for not only his leadership ability and dedication to his academics, but also for his determination to be a HS educator. His mother and I spoke about his recent work and his continued commitment to teach at Apollo HS one of these days. She also mentioned that she was sad to see me retire but that she also understood. Once again, it was good to hear from someone outside of the daily Apollo HS "grind" mention that I made an influence on not only her, but also her son. I told her that it was a pleasure working with her and having her son in school and that I expected to see her son before this year ends (if he would be willing to stop by and pay a visit). She mentioned that she would be happy to pass that on....

Despite the uneasy feeling that I have about the conditions of the last four weeks of my career, one thing that keeps me going are the "glimmers of hope" like Lauren and this recent Apollo graduate, who will soon be in the trenches making an impact on the future of society.

April 26, 2022 - I have avoided mentioning the continued troubles that we have had in the behavior of our students in this Spring Semester. While the overall behavior of our students has improved, we are still seeing more than the usual fights that are breaking out among students. We are seeing more students vaping and/or selling vape "supplies" than usual, and we continue to have issues with our student attendance. Moving forward, these are issues that the new administration will have to continue to work through and also find solutions to help diminish them. At this point in the year (in my *career*), there is nothing more that Rick Lasley can do about it....

Another very disappointing trend that continues to plague the current educators in the trenches today is how much the legislators have all but forgotten about them when considering "infrastructure" needs and adequate funding for pay raises and training. In the last legislative session, it was decided for state employees to have an eight percent increase in pay this next fiscal year with the promise of a twelve percent increase in pay the following year. That is all well and good; I am quite certain that these state employees are *long* overdue for these raises! The only problem with this is that educators are not included. The state of Kentucky did agree to raise the per pupil funding for school districts where most will be able to consider a two percent or three percent increase in staff pay this next year. While this **IS** a good thing, it pales in comparison to what is desperately needed to get the teacher salaries back to where they should be... **DESERVE** to be...! Thinking back over my thirty-two year career, I cannot remember the last time we had more than a one percent raise....

It is quite depressing when you think about how educators' pay, lack of society's respect for the profession, and the reduced number of applicants in the pipeline has gotten to the point that it has today. How could the legislators "pass" each year on providing the adequate funding that school districts need to provide the "free public education for all" that our founding fathers guaranteed in developing our rights as citizens? Once again, it boggles my mind considering what is at stake when we poorly invest in the education of our youth. Let's see... Do we want the future of our society here in America adequately prepared by highly motivated and qualified teachers? On the other hand, do we want to gamble and poorly equip our schools to provide the future of our society for what they need to be successful because we cannot guarantee that certified teachers will be teaching them? Unbelievable! Yet, here we are....

Moving on... One of the tasks that I have been working to complete this week is all of the Classified Employee evaluations. This is an important task for me to be sure and pass on to the next principal by ensuring that all evaluations include very authentic feedback. Too many times, a retiring principal will "pass" everyone on their way out. While some of the "go-getters" and "Rock Stars" are given the challenge to criticize their own work, I want to ensure that I leave feedback for ALL employees that will give them what they need to consider as improvement goals going into next year.

This week, I have completed all of the custodian evaluations and have had the conference with each one of them. While this has been a VERY challenging year for this group (considering how long we went in the fall semester with four positions of eleven **unfilled**), we still have expectations for proper cleanliness of the building and grounds. For two of our newly hired custodians, we need to leave them with the understanding that they must improve their overall attitude and work ethic.

In the very least, insubordination (not following through with a task given by a supervisor) will not at all be tolerated. Even with the shortage of individuals in these positions, it is better to do without one than to have a custodian that you have to follow behind to make sure they are doing what they are supposed to!

April 27, 2022 (Secretaries Day) - This is a day that we pay tribute to the **real** "bosses" of the schools that we operate. I have had my share of administrative professionals (secretaries) over my twenty-year span as an administrator, and every one of them has been overworked and underappreciated. These individuals, whom I have had the pleasure to work with at Apollo HS, have each been responsible in making it the special place that it is. Because this was my last opportunity to do so, I wanted to let them each know how much their work and dedication meant to me....

We have a total of nine individuals who would be considered in the "Secretary" category between the main office, guidance office, library, and attendance office. With the recent construction and new building, the main office and attendance office are split and on opposite ends of the building, making it hard for the groups to maintain any form of connection that used to exist. For each of the locations, I put in an order for some breakfast cakes (scones, muffins, cookies) so that these individuals would be able to enjoy some treats with their morning coffee. While a lot of schools do this for their secretaries (and maybe more), this was **my** gesture to them for their hard work and support **of my work** over the past six years. The school was still making the annual gesture of a hanging pot of flowers arranged from our Ag Horticulture class to each of these nine individuals. They certainly deserve that and then some....

These past two days I have been able to help cashier at lunch and make some connections with students. As always, it has been a refreshing break from being stuck in the office going over evaluations or any other item I have been tasked with. While this job has been a lifesaver for me this year, and I know that the ladies have appreciated my help a GREAT deal (as they mention almost daily), this is something that will not last. It is just inconceivable to be a task that the new principal can or will even be **willing** to consistently fill. While I hope that the ladies find themselves NOT needing the assistance moving forward, I hope there are other options made available to them when they do. The new principal will have his/her hands full in other areas of the building for sure....

Today also marked my **last** official Faculty Meeting. In this meeting, I went over details for the important dates and events leading up to the last day of school and graduation. I made sure that the teachers knew when the state assessment days were and also who would be responsible for proctoring the exams. With the fifteen days of school that are left (can that be correct?), there is an event or a deadline on EVERY single day that the teachers need to be made aware. I had to take this opportunity to explain the importance of the grading deadlines for seniors and also our underclassmen at the end of the year. We also explained how we would work out our closing day and what has become a make-up day that we didn't see coming....

One of the more frustrating things that I have noticed as a veteran educator (and I likewise have had conversations with other veteran educators) is the reluctance and complaints to fulfill duties that **come with teaching** that can sometimes be heard from teachers today. Fulfilling your Closing Day as a contractual day of work and the fact that ALL teachers are supposed to attend Graduation are two perfect examples. BOTH of these are items that **come with the job** and are contractual obligations, yet too many of our educators today are finding ways to get out of those duties.

At my last faculty meeting, I left them all with the best advice that I could leave them:

- DO NOT take any aspect of your jobs as educators for granted. Take pleasure in ALL the items that make being an educator unique – especially the HIGH SCHOOL Graduation…!
- If you want the respect and appeal to ever come back to the education profession, you must (without fail) be prepared to uphold the professionalism that comes with the job…!

Only time will tell if this advice is taken….

April 29, 2022 (New Principal announced at Apollo HS) - On Wednesday of this week, interviews for the new principal of Apollo HS took place, with the decision taking place yesterday. TODAY there is a special SBDM Council meeting to make the decision official and announce the new principal at Apollo HS (effective July 1 of this year). The staff and public are all invited to attend the meeting.

Since my bizarre rant last week, I have made the decision that *I am in complete control of my emotions and state of mind* as I end my career (regardless of what may exist or what is going on around me). I can either make the most of my last days, or I can choose a path that would leave a lasting negative effect on me and those around me. The latter is not at all the lasting impression that I want to leave as any part of my legacy, if there is one. What will make my remaining days most difficult is the feeling that I am "in the way" for the work being done for the future of Apollo and that time will start to crawl….

Today we hosted a very "normal" Career Fair for our seniors in the auxiliary gym, and it was attended by all of the regional business and career partners within a given distance of Owensboro. Our CCR Team did their usual stellar job in lining up these partners and especially connecting certain students with businesses or industry partners who will make a perfect match. "Dynamos" at work! It was awesome to hear that some of our EL seniors were set up to visit a local industry partner that was in need of summer help. This was a win-win scenario where both parties came away with what was needed. One of many things that I am VERY proud of in our work at Apollo HS is the emphasis on EVERY EAGLE, EVERY DAY and the fact that we individualize the needs of every student. Our CCR Team is a perfect example of a group that makes this philosophy part of their mantra. **KUDOS** to their work and dedication to the students at Apollo HS…!

I have been making the most of my remaining moments as I walk around the building and connect with staff and students. We had a fun moment among "us" cafeteria ladies when I stopped by to check in on them. It is pretty cool that they consider me one of the group when they share a moment while they are "roasting" one of the crew. It is good to see the smiles and laughs, and it is even better to be made a part of the fun.

Students will stop me on occasion in passing to mention that they heard I was retiring (or to ask). Each time the students will say that they will miss me or ask if I can stay on for "one more year." To these comments, I tell them I appreciate their words, and I mention how much I will miss them as well. THIS is truly what I will miss the most— the connections I have been able to make over the years with the students. SO MUCH has changed about the students and there are A LOT more headaches that we have to deal with these days compared to twenty years ago. Even though they STILL drive us bonkers at times, we love them and nonetheless want what is best for them. We educators do our best to guide EVERY student on the path that will lead them to success and the ability to contribute positively to society. Not all of them follow our guidance and not all of them are successful, but it remains to be our life's mission to make a difference with EVERY child that we can. For all the ones who DO make it, their story becomes the fuel to keep us going in an effort to help the next one....

At the Special-called SBDM Meeting and announcement regarding the new Principal of Apollo HS, it was made official that one of my assistant principals would be taking over as leader of Apollo HS effective July 1, 2022. For a short-notice announcement and especially at 4:00 on a Friday afternoon, I was pleased that a vast majority of the Apollo Staff and a good number of district staff made their presence known to show support for this transition. The new leader of Apollo gave his inaugural speech, making a good impression for the new era. He has certainly worked hard for this moment over the past twelve years serving in his role as assistant principal. I wish him and Apollo HS all the best moving forward....

May 3, 2022 - State Testing started today for 10th and 11th graders. This is the first year that schools are being held accountable for *all* students in those grade levels being tested since the pandemic began in March 2020. For schools like Apollo HS who have battled poor attendance all year and have had the lingering issues of lost learning for algebra coupled with motivation and engagement issues with students, the adults can't help but feel a little anxious about the pending results. It would be nice to get EVERY student into the school at least by make-up testing and be held accountable at the very least to TAKE the assessments they are responsible for. I am afraid that THIS year will present a challenge to accomplish that task.

On the good side of assessment day, Apollo HS is like a well-oiled machine! Those responsible for setting up the assessment by splitting the students up with a location to test and an adult proctor to complete the task, not to mention all of the students who require testing accommodations, make it look so simple. Although I know that these adults are a little anxious on the inside to get everyone where they are supposed to go (students AND proctors) and each group logged in and started on time, they certainly do not show it on the outside. The ladies in the Guidance Office are PROS at setting up assessments ("Rock Stars" in their **own** right) and especially in expediting the mate- rials with the human resources moving in all the right directions. They have had practice at this gig, for sure, but they have done a marvelous job encompassing the continuous improvement model in their method each year and have worked out all the kinks. With the help and assistance of the Building Assessment Coordinators (BAC), this entire team of individuals do a **marvelous** job... with ZERO influence or direction from their principal... it just happens!

The ONE item I may help with after the first day of assessment is tracking the absences of students and what exams they missed. Ultimately, we want to ensure ALL students (or as many as possible) are held accountable for their testing sessions. Again, this is a very tall task, but well worth any effort or manpower put into it....

Aside from the state assessment procedures that consumed our day today, the volume of people who are reaching out to me regarding my retirement has increased since the announcement of the new principal at Apollo HS. This past weekend I had a former student reach out to congratulate me on my retirement and to tell me that I was "an awesome principal." This student was a senior my first year at Apollo and my first Principal's Leadership Award recipient. This incredible student had the dedication, work ethic, poise, and determination to lead an army but settled for carrying our volleyball team on her shoulders as Apollo waltzed through the 3rd Region Tournament as champions. She graduated with her college degree one year ago and is already paving her path by making a positive influence on the people with whom she connects. To hear from anyone regarding my retirement in this manner is uplifting, but to hear from students like her really means a lot....

On top of messages from former students, I still have the occasional "Congratulations, Mr. Lasley" in the hallway as I pass by students. Earlier today, one of our most challenging students made this comment to me. While it may not have had the same impact on me as to hear from my former student, I could tell by the smile on his face that it was a very genuine gesture. That THIS student made a point to say anything to me in this manner was very much appreciated, and I made sure to tell him just that....

I also received a very special card from a very special person to me. One of our day custodians is also retiring at the end of this year. She has had a wild ride these past two years with surgery on both knees. Before that, it was hard for her to get around and perform her normal duties as a custodian. But you never would hear her complain! She performed her duties as best she could, considering the limitations that her knees presented, and went out of her way to perform tasks that were needed without being asked. I can recall on several mornings walking through the "Dome" area back to the office after ENL, telling her "the area looks good/smells good!" She would say "thanks," and we would bid each other a "good day" and move on about our work. It is moments like this that I will remember moving forward. My hope is that this custodian enjoys the time she will have after retirement with her new knees and the ability to get around without pain or struggle....

The last good word that was shared was by my superintendent. In an email exchange that started out with a completely different intention, he commended me for the professional approach that I was giving in "passing of the baton" to the next principal of Apollo HS. This meant a lot to hear, along with the personal message he shared. These connections I have made in the past forty-eight hours have been uplifting and very affirming for the time I have given over my career. I can only hope this trend continues over the next ten days that remain in this school year...!

May 5, 2022 (Senior Honors Night) - This time of year in high schools across the nation is all about the seniors as they complete their education and enter adulthood, whether they are ready for it or not. I have always enjoyed seeing high school students transform from the shy and awkward freshmen as they enter high school into the young adults that they are by the time they walk across the stage at graduation. For some, it is quite the metamorphosis, very similar to the drastic change from a caterpillar to a butterfly. For me, I enjoy seeing the students who have had to work the hardest to overcome adversity on their way through high school— some having to learn from mistakes early on and some just struggling more than others for a variety of reasons. For **these** students, I cannot help but to beam inside when I see them cross the stage and especially anytime I see them after graduation, knowing that they are contributing in a positive way to society. THAT is what defines the experience as a high school educator, and it has been a part of my life for the past thirty-two years...!

Yesterday, our seniors had a Field Day (designed by three of our physical education teachers) that was composed of several physical activities on our turf football field. Other than the event itself, what made this experience awesome was that the idea came from our seniors leaders. The president of the senior class stopped by my office just before Spring Break and pitched the idea of not only this Field Day but also other activities that would define the last twenty-two days of the school year (22 for the Class of 2022…). Other than Field Day, the vast majority of the activities would not interfere with the school day but would be fun activities that would help the seniors make their last days at Apollo HS more memorable. WHY NOT…? Once again, as I have mentioned before, these moments make the very BEST part of my job!

Tonight, we honored the seniors who will be graduating with some form of distinction, either earning a special scholarship, earning the label of Honor Graduate, or earning a spot among the Senior Sweet 16. THESE students are among the best of the best at Apollo HS, and I could not help but see each one of them as another "glimmer of hope" for the future of society (and, YES, a handful electing to pursue education!), each one of them possessing talents and character traits that will successfully take them wherever they choose to go. IF ONLY, we could get MORE of our students to fall into this category….Normally, once I acknowledge to myself "this will be my last ___," I can't help but lose myself in thought and consider a little emotion. Tonight, I focused on the tasks that I was responsible for and made the most of them. In my introduction, I took advantage of the first public opportunity to congratulate the assistant principal who would be the next principal of Apollo, and I allowed him to finish out the introduction. At the end of the ninety-minute ceremony, I also took advantage of recognizing the teachers and other staff members who were present. The dedication and determination of these adults, especially over the course of these past two years, helped shape these seniors into who they are today, and I offered the students and their families an opportunity to thank them for their work. A vast majority of the adults who were present tonight to give awards or to witness the senior honors are true "Rock Stars." Those **not** considered in this category (in **my** mind, at least) are on their way there.

As Apollo Principal, my very last responsibility for Honors Night is to recognize the Honor Graduate (the ONE senior who will address their classmates at the Graduation Ceremony) and also the senior that I choose to receive the Principal's Leadership Award. Even before I came to Apollo, I have always taken pleasure in the writing of the words to describe the transformation that takes place in the student that I recognize – from the person that started as a freshman, the adversity they may have battled, and the person now standing before us. In my description, I am always careful not to mention their name until near the very end – letting the "suspense" build for the crowd but also allowing the individual a moment to identify themselves in my words before anyone else. MAN… What a ***thrill***!

As I finish this journal entry, I cannot help but think back over the senior classes that I have graduated and the individuals that I have personally awarded. It has ***truly*** been an honor to be a part of this experience for the past thirty-two years! Whether any honor has been reciprocated by any student or adult I have come into contact with is irrelevant… I am at peace….

May 6, 2022 ("O me, O life!") - This Friday was a blur as I had a lot on my mind that kept my attention from anything Apollo. Today, Lauren graduates from the University of Kentucky with her Bachelor of Arts in Music Education degree, and I cannot think of much else. Because there were several of the Leadership Team who were occupied with testing and other tasks, we had a condensed version of our weekly meeting with just the administrators. The topics were seniors NOT graduating and the list of tenth and eleventh graders who needed to be tracked down next week for make-up testing. For any student who fails to complete the assessment, we take a "0" and that will not bode well with our school's accountability measures….

It's hard to imagine that we have been tracking our "Seniors-N-Danger" since the beginning of this semester, running seven failure reports, following up with conferences with the seniors and sometimes their parents, and yet we STILL have sixteen seniors who are potentially NOT graduating because of failed credits in required classes. At this moment, four seniors will not graduate and will have to attend summer school to earn their diploma. By the middle of next week, I fully expect that this list will be more than double.

After securing all the items I needed to accomplish for the week, I got on the road to pick up Angela and Troy to head for Lexington. As we made the two-and-a-half hour journey, my mind went back to my graduation at the same university thirty-two years ago almost to the day. I can remember those feelings that I had, ready to embark on a new journey in finding a job and making my own way. I am very proud of Lauren for many reasons, and I can only imagine the same things that are going through her mind as well....

The university president gave an eloquent address to the graduates, and I was pleased to hear him reference Walt Whitman's poem, "O Me! O Life," as it is partly responsible for steering me on my path to become an educator. Not that I am an avid reader of poetry, but the poem was featured in the 1988 movie *Dead Poets Society* starring Robin Williams as "Mr. Keating." If my mind wasn't completely sure if teaching was for me, it was firmly etched in granite at the point that I saw the movie at the university "cinema" in the spring of my sophomore year. This movie had such an impact on my decisions and the longing to **BE** the impact on the students that I connected with that I had the following excerpt from Walt Whitman's poem printed and framed. It has been hanging on my office wall for the past twenty years:

...that the powerful play goes on

*and that **YOU***

may contribute a verse.

What will your verse be?

Call it sentimental, call it corny, but I find it poetic (no pun intended) that I have come **full circle** sitting at the graduation ceremony of my daughter who has chosen a path as an educator thirty-two years after my own graduation at my alma mater..., AND this poem is featured in the university president's address. Chills....

The worst part of the experience was that the individual calling the graduate's names as they crossed the stage somehow mispronounced our last name. Lasley somehow became "Lay-Zee" and the expression on Lauren's face as well as the expletive words that came out of my mouth said it all. Even with this unfortunate mishap, we didn't let it detract us from the experience and the family making it known to Lauren just how proud we were of her. This picture is one of **many** that we took to commemorate this special moment in our family. Two Lasley educators (pronounced "LAY-Zee" by the University of Kentucky) – one soon to retire, another soon to be hired...What an AWESOME day...!

May 10, 2022 - I woke up yesterday to find an email from the parent of another school in the area complaining of "threats" being made by one of Apollo's parents via text. Both parents' children participate in one of our spring sports teams. This parent **expected** a response from me as well as the Kentucky High School Athletic Association (KHSAA) as to what we were going to do about it. I have mentioned before the irrational parents who fully expect administrators to "police" harassing/bullying/threatening messages that are sent between students on the weekends and during the summers. I have now seen and heard it all if this parent expects that I am going to "punish" this Apollo **parent** OR hold the **child** of the parent accountable for what the parent communicates in a text. *Are you kidding me??*

Back in the world of reality and on a much more positive note, I am very pleased to report that I was WRONG. In the early stages of my first journal that led to the publishing of *Humanity in Peril*, my concerns for the conditions that we were working through at the beginning of this year prompted my prediction that **even more** teachers would be retiring or moving on at the end of this year compared to May 2021. As of the writing of this journal entry, we have the same number moving on to other pursuits in education or retiring as we did last year (nine total counting teachers, principal, and support staff). While this is considered above average for any given year, at least it is not MORE. With pandemic conditions continuing to get better (let's all hope, at least!), maybe... just MAYBE... the early exit for educators will be stabilized. This time next year we will know the answer....

Another "glimmer of hope" that at least Apollo HS has witnessed is the movement of veteran educators willing to apply for our open teaching positions. WE HAVE APPLICANTS for every open position and have made some quality hires at this point, that is, with the exception of science. Unfortunately, we have two positions to fill, and we have ZERO certified applicants. This has been very common across the state of Kentucky for science....

Although I mentioned that Apollo has had quality and veteran applicants for our other open positions, this is only making a void in the schools that they are leaving. My hope is that those schools have applicants to fill those positions. It only makes sense that we cannot just trade teachers to achieve equilibrium and perfect harmony in education. We NEED eligible first-year teacher candidates for EVERY teacher who retires moving forward for the future of education to remain stable. *If only the communities and our elected officials can come to their senses and do what is necessary to fully fund education over the next three or four years!* Time will tell... the clock IS ticking...!

One item I have been battling here lately is the fact that **the work is moving past me**. This cannot be helped at the point that the new principal has been named for next school year and is working in the same building. My initial goal to **work up until the very end** of the school year is just not possible. Beyond the work at my desk to finish up evaluations, track down student absences from state assessment, conference with seniors who just CANNOT help themselves, and any other end of year paperwork, I find myself feeling that I am "in the way." My concerns are that this feeling will only INCREASE as each day passes and will certainly be the case at the point that graduation is over. I have three more weeks of work to put in, and I find myself boxing some things up to take up my time. While that is a necessary task at some point, it does not help my feeling that my time is pretty much done. Moving forward, I need to do a better job of occupying my time and find other places than my office to be....

One good thing that has happened since the announcement of my replacement has been my replacement stopping by from time to time to ask questions or my opinion about scenarios moving forward. While I do not expect this to continue to happen, he did not have to do it at all. That he HAS done this the times he has means a lot....

My last responsibility as the Chair of the Apollo SBDM Council took place today at the regular May meeting. For Apollo HS, the by-laws state that the last regular meeting for the year is in May, and currently, no **regular** meeting is scheduled in June. I am glad this one is over for the same reasons that I mentioned earlier. The work of the SBDM Council is certainly moving WELL past me. My only hope is that they appreciate the time that I have given as not only the chair for the council, but also as the principal of Apollo HS for the past six years. As of the time that the meeting ended, I have been given no indication that is the case....

This evening, I tried to split time between two events going on. Because we do not have access to our auditorium (in the process of being renovated), our Spring Choir and Band Concerts had to be held off- campus at the Bluegrass Museum downtown. It is also our last home baseball game before district tournament begins and senior night to recognize our baseball seniors. Both events started at the same time, so I decided to start out at the choir and band concerts to spend my last opportunity with those performers and then go to the baseball game an hour late (those games always last well beyond two hours anyway).

It is **always** a pleasure to see and hear our students perform, and this concert was no different. Because of the acoustics at the museum and the prominence of the venue itself, the students were outstanding! I was able to witness the entire choir performance and hear the band play their first song before I had to leave. The concert band is led by two dynamic directors who have both been instrumental in moving the band in a positive direction, despite the conditions of these past two years. The choir instructor has done a **phenomenal** job increasing the choir membership two-fold, as well as the musicianship of her performers. EVERY public performance of our band and choir is a testament to the credibility of the adults, as well as the hard work of all involved. I am happy to have made the decision to attend this event... It made my day!

I arrived back to campus just as the third inning had ended with Apollo enjoying a comfortable lead over their opponent. Before the game concluded, the Eagles managed to "run-rule" their opponent (achieving a 10-run lead after the fifth inning). Overall, it was a VERY good day to be an Eagle...!

May 12, 2022 - This week I had the pleasure of joining the Intro to Education class to check in on them and to also give them an opportunity to ask any "parting" questions that they may have regarding my plans after retirement. In the course of this conversation, I inquired which students had plans to pursue education as a career. As I recall from the first time I asked the question earlier this year, fewer hands seemed to raise (by two or three), but a good number still remained. I also reinforced the fact that it was okay to start college and be unsure exactly what you wanted to do. I relayed my experience going to college for the first time, thinking that I was going to eventually apply and be accepted in the school of architecture. Whether it **could** have happened at all, it doesn't matter. By the time I had finished my sophomore year, I had completely grounded myself to pursue what would be my passion.

These students were receptive to the advice that I gave, and their "Rock Star" teacher followed up with some questions of her own. I asked each senior where they intended to go to school the following year and what their intended course of study would be. I wished them each the very best of luck, and I was out the door to find something else to occupy my mind....

Today I had the pleasure of having my last summative evaluation conference with an individual who had spent these past two pandemic years with us. Because of the conditions we have all worked through, I feel, in fairness, that it had a negative effect on the influence this individual has demonstrated around Apollo. Rather than simply giving this person a "pass" of an evaluation, I made certain to give them the very best advice I could give in an effort to help them on their way to success in their role next year. I made sure to communicate what I intended to share with this individual with both administrators because it would be **their** responsibility to evaluate this individual moving forward. At the end of the conference, we both agreed on what was discussed, and this individual thanked me for being open and honest in my feedback. To have done anything else would have been a total waste of time....

One of the best parts of my time this week has been spent visiting EL classrooms with Apollo's "Dynamo" EL Instructional Coach to deliver certificates to students who had increased their ACCESS scores from the year before. We decided to make these presentations a big deal by presenting each student with a laminated certificate (including the principal's signature!) in front of their peers. Much like the visits we made to classrooms earlier this week, the visit we made to one of the EL classrooms today was an awesome experience! The students recognized our appreciation and pride and even received applause from their classmates. After taking a group photo of the students with their teacher and me, the IC gave the class one last pep-talk about working hard so that hopefully each one of them would be able to receive a certificate next year! We will see if this pans out and proves to make more students successful on the ACCESS test. Whether it does or does not, these students *each* were very deserving of this recognition!

One of the greatest "glimmer of hope" moments for education that has happened in a LONG time took place at the special-called DCPS Board Meeting this evening. The board members took the recommendation of giving ALL employees a three percent raise this next school year! This amount of a raise has not happened more than a couple of times over my thirty-two year career. The vast majority of the raises I have experienced were either zero percent or one percent. It has been a minimum of fifteen years since a raise has been any different. Regardless, **THIS IS GOOD NEWS** for what I hope (for ALL) is only the beginning. I also hope that there is something similar that is being planned in other districts across the state… **BRAVO** DCPS!

May 16, 2022 (*LAST* Monday) - In an effort to enter the last week of school a little more casual than usual, I declared a Luau Monday at

Apollo HS and asked the adults to wear a Hawaiin shirt or luau attire. At least with students in the building, this would be my **last** Monday of my career as an educator. With seniors out of the building at the start of the day and the rest of the students in review mode for final exams, it already felt a little awkward....

Over the past ten years or more as a principal, I have taken on a project at the end of each year that I have thoroughly enjoyed. In the midst of closing out each year and preparing for the graduation ceremony, I have found it to be very therapeutic to gather pictures taken from special events over the year and put them together in a slideshow with three songs of my choosing that define the "tone" for the year. Sometimes the lyrics have a special message that also describe moments that have made that particular year unlike any other year. At the very end of the video, I include past and present pictures of our retirees to honor them and wish them the best of luck moving forward. I show this video at the year end celebration, and the staff have always enjoyed the "Year-N-Review" moments as the timeline for that year is unveiled.

Because I had little else to do on this day (none of my work would be moving beyond graduation in three days), I spent some time sorting the pictures and building the video with all the moments that made this year what it was. I have always paid careful attention to the adults who have had children over the course of this year, and I make sure to insert some of the first baby pics with the baby's name included within the video. The best parts are when we have had a comical moment that was captured on video or just a comical moment I have made up to poke a little fun with an adult or two who are known to share some fun-loving themselves. The reaction of the audience always affirms when I have hit the target....

With this "Year-N-Review" video being my last, I would like for it to be as good or better than any I have produced before, but I am short on very many fun-loving moments, and I am battling what to do to recognize my own retirement when I have spent thirty-two years either just off stage or standing **behind** the spotlight. I have not been prepared to make this part of the video, and I am finding that my retirement recognition is taking the enjoyment that I usually have out of the production. As of the end of this day, I am ready to set the video aside and let it "marinade" a little, while asking a few people for pictures of events that have happened over the year that are missing in my stockpile. Maybe the video will come together better over the next couple of days....

Tomorrow is Primary Election Day in Kentucky, which means there will be no school for students. Adults will all be in the building making up some work from one of the days missed over the course of this year. This will be our last opportunity to work with teachers or have the teachers work in their departments. Each of the teachers will also be given opportunities to finalize some grades so that the deadline is met to have ALL grades posted and FINAL by 3:00 pm this Thursday. If the weather is kind to us, Graduation for the Class of 2022 will take place Thursday night at the football stadium starting at 6:30 pm. We are closely monitoring a rain event that predicted will wash out Wednesday and finish up early Thursday in the Owensboro area. Time will tell....

May 18, 2022 (*LAST* Last Day of School) - As bad fortune would have it, the weather patterns for this evening did not look hopeful based on the morning weather forecast that I watched before heading to work. The morning weather would at least allow us the opportunity to practice one last time with the seniors on the football field. Yesterday, because of rain showers off and on all day, the first graduation practice had to be held in our main gymnasium. Although it was awkward to envision the set-up and arrangement of the ceremony in a much smaller space, the seniors were patient and well-behaved through the entire practice.

Not long after practice was over yesterday, I was in my office picking up where I left off with the "Year-N-Review" video when I was paid a very special visit by a very special group of ladies. All sixteen of our cafeteria ladies filed into my office with a gift bag and some forlorn looks on their faces. They had gotten me a couple of gifts, and they all wanted me to spend one last moment with them. One gift was the picture that I took with them a few weeks ago, framed and with white formatting. Each one of the ladies had written a special message to me, wishing me well in retirement or thanking me for my help. The second gift was a handmade and embroidered denim apron with the words "ALL STAR Lunch Lady" over the Apollo Eagle mascot.

It goes without saying that these ladies had me fighting back tears, and the sentiment was returned as I shared with them one last time how much my time with them this year **saved** me. It wasn't just the connections with the kids that made my time spent at lunch an uplifting experience, it was also in getting to know each of them better and just enjoying their company. There were days that I felt like one of them! It's gifts like the ones the ladies shared with me that are special and can never be forgotten. The time I spent this year working as a cashier at lunch was priceless. Before our moment was complete yesterday, I received sixteen hugs with one last message and a photo taken with me and my new apron. As quietly as they all walked in, they all turned and filed out one by one from my office. **THAT** moment would be a hard one to beat in my last moments as an educator...!

Both today and yesterday were Final Exam days with a special schedule arranged for review before each exam was taken. None of the seniors are in the building on these days because of their graduation practices and other events, so the population is already reduced by one-fourth. Some of the other students have also earned final exam exemptions that allow them to miss part of the day (show up late or leave early). Due to this, the school day just doesn't have the same feel. Teachers are busy grading final exams and getting the grades entered into the gradebook immediately afterward. The students that remain in the building are mostly up to mischief being in places they shouldn't be and being tracked down by the assistant principals. None of this makes for any memorable moments for an educator's *last* last day of school. I had plenty of work to occupy my time in my office, and one important item on my list today was to be on a three-way call with the director of Daviess County EMS and one of the meteorologists at the national weather service....

The information shared by them was not good, as they relayed that the weather patterns were upgraded to an enhanced risk in our area for hail, strong winds, and storms. There were two systems coming through that would potentially hit Owensboro with one system arriving just prior to the ceremony and a stronger one coming through a couple hours later. As with ANY weather forecast, this one was not one-hundred percent, and it would be scattered. Nonetheless, we all agreed that the risk of trying to have graduation that night was not at all worth finding out. With this information in hand, I reached out to the superintendent that we would have to move the graduation ceremony to tomorrow night. At that point, we both worked to make sure the information was communicated appropriately within the school, to families, and throughout the community.

Because this day did not have a graduation ceremony at the end of the evening for me to make final preparations for, I took the opportunity to gather my things after the school day ended to head home a little earlier than normal....

May 20, 2022 (Graduation) - As it typically happens when you cancel a large outdoor event based on weather patterns in late May, it did not storm or rain at any point last night, which would have kept us from having the graduation ceremony. **However**, it certainly looked like it could rain at any time, and again, based on the forecast that we received directly from the National Weather Service, it was not worth taking the risk.

Because we had Project Graduation last night, due to the prior booking of entertainment that could not be rescheduled, and in order to allow those adults in the building who attended a bit of extra rest, we started our Closing Day activities at 8:30 am. Based on the looks of those who were at the event last night, I could tell that they did not get much sleep. For the first part of the morning, all teachers were to ensure that they had all their course grades in order and FINAL. They also had to get their rooms boxed up to prepare for a move to another part of the building (continued renovations to start in the "300" section next week) OR ensure everything was secure so that the summer custodial crews could start the summer cleaning process. Either way, the teachers had some work to do for Closing Day.

At 10:00 am, we had the annual Year-end Celebration and Retiree Recognition set to take place. With everyone back in the Commons Area, we took time for the Board Member representatives who joined us to give their presentations to all six retirees (including me). The board chairman happens to be a former Apollo High School principal himself, so he always shares a story about each one of the retirees (at least the ones he had worked with or hired when he was principal). Either way, it is good to have this perspective for the audience to be able to connect each retiree's beginning as an educator. At the point that I received my award from the board members, it suddenly became real that my career was about to end.

After the board members gave their presentations, each department that had a retiring member typically puts together a skit or at least a presentation. With the talented bunch that Apollo HS has, it is not uncommon to have a popular song played with the lyrics rewritten to suit the individual and their personality. This is always a treat and good for several laughs as the retiree is in the spotlight.

The skits that are performed typically involve all members of the department, and the theme is based upon funny events that have transpired over the years or just the habits that the individual has that may or may not be exaggerated. Once again, the routine is appreciated very much by the crowd, and the retiree always appreciates the sentiment and the "good fun" that was shared at their expense. This Apollo tradition is one like no other I have ever witnessed and one of a handful of reasons that Apollo HS is the special place that it is.

As we went through each of the other five retirees, I emceed as I normally do as the principal of the school. For each one, I always have some personal words to share of my own. After giving the respects to each of the other retiring members, it was suddenly my turn, and my secretary had to take over the microphone.

Like the other retiring members, I held it together quite well, and we all kept our emotions in check (for the most part). Although it is hard to consider that your career is ending, it is not nearly as hard when you know you are DONE and are ready to move on. That, at least, is where I am and what I have been feeling for the past couple of months as this school year has come to a close....

All in all, it was a great ceremony, with the appropriate amount of recognition given to each of the retirees. The audience gave each one of the retirees a personal standing ovation at the end of each recognition. I greatly appreciated seeing that gesture, and I know each of the other retirees felt the same. In the end, we were all gifted a variation of rocking chairs, "gag" retirement gifts, t-shirts, money, gift cards, and the like. The Eagle Family spared no expense in gathering money for the other retirees and me. Several hugs and handshakes were passed around as well. The individual conversations at the end were the ones that meant the most to me. Those who revered our work the most or the ones who we worked closest with shared genuine words that made the very best gifts of all.

At the conclusion of the recognition, we watched my final "Year-N-Review" video for 2022 and had lunch that was donated by Papa Grande's. It was a **GOOD** day to end your career....

We knew it was supposed to be windy, but we were not at all prepared for how windy it was as Angela and I entered the stadium. The florist, our head custodian, and the senior guidance counselor had the worst time trying to keep everything standing. The flower arrangements were all weighed down, and with nowhere to go, the flowers were shredding! Thankfully, the placement of some artificial flowers within the arrangements kept them looking "full," and the wind also started dying down about thirty minutes before the program started.

Beyond that, it was a perfect evening for a graduation ceremony. The crowd was beyond capacity by the time the ceremony started, with the stands full and the straggling spectators all standing around the fence surrounding the field. The speeches were given and the diplomas were distributed by the board members and the superintendent. After twenty years of giving speeches to graduating classes, these were the words I chose to share with the Apollo HS Class of 2022:

> *Apollo High School Class of 2022, HERE WE ARE... You and I are about to "hit the road" and leave Apollo HS one last time. YES, I KNOW, it's an EERIE feeling, and I can attest to the same bittersweet emotions that many of you are feeling. In this last graduation ceremony for me, I hope to ease your minds a little and leave you one last bit of advice....*

Sitting at my HS graduation ceremony 36 years ago, I had no idea what direction I was headed. My mind had thoughts of journalism and more likely architecture (using my strong math ability), but I can tell you that the last thing on my mind was becoming a teacher.

By the time I finished my first year in college, I realized that I could NOT be happy pursuing anything that did not directly tie me to public service and shaping the lives of young adults. As corny as it may sound, it was the movie Dead Poets Society that made my decision to pursue education vividly clear. This movie and its characters SPOKE TO MY HEART and allowed me to FIND MY PASSION. I started teaching in August of 1990, and I stand before you today 32 years later giving this address to Apollo HS's Class of 2022. If Rick Lasley, a country boy who grew up in White Mills, KY can achieve what I have, then EACH one of you can do the same... Here is the SUMMARY to your SUCCESS:

- ALWAYS be true to yourself. DO NOT let anyone tell you who you should be or what you should become. THAT is a question only YOU can answer.
- Follow YOUR HEART and FIND YOUR PASSION. As much as I would give you explicit instructions for how this will happen, I'm sorry, I can't. I WILL say that it will become VIVIDLY clear to you at the moment that you realize it.
- WORK HARD - especially when the work BECOMES HARD. Nothing defines work ethic MORE than those who give up when the work gets hard.
- STAY POSITIVE and BE KIND to everyone you connect with. We all know there is FAR too much hate and negativity in the world. Please help become a part of the GOOD that this world has to offer.

Apollo Graduating Class of 2022 -YOU have made the Eagle Family

*PROUD for making it to this moment. No matter what may take place in the coming years, please know that Apollo is here to help you as you continue your journey and that you will **ALWAYS be a member of the Eagle Family**....*

May 25, 2022 - The work of a retiring principal is minimal at best when you get beyond the Closing Day of the school year and graduation. Due to this, I was going to make this one last journal entry with some parting thoughts to share as my career ends, but my heart is *weeping,* and I cannot finish this book without paying tribute. My "parting thoughts" will have to come later....

Nineteen innocent children and two courageous adults lost their lives yesterday in Uvalde, Texas. This horrendous act happened on Awards Day and just two days before the end of the school year at Robb Elementary School. While the battle between gun-control advocates and their opponents rages on, there are two facts that everyone seems to be missing or overlooking: that guns will **ALWAYS** be available for the deviant people who want to use them for horrendous purpose AND there is not enough being done to find the help for the growing number of mental health issues that exist in our nation today! Our schools are NOT safe enough if events like what took place in Uvalde, Texas continue to happen...!

No matter where you are today, May 25, 2022, you **HAVE TO** be saddened by the innocent lives that were lost yesterday. Whether this statement is true or not, I can tell you that *educators* across the nation are in *mourning*. Our schools SHOULD BE the safest place for our children to be, especially our elementary school children. Yet, in just shy of ten years time, we had twenty-six lives lost in Sandy Hook Elementary in Connecticut (December 2012) and now the twenty-one lives lost yesterday at Robb Elementary in Texas. How much longer before these events STOP happening? Is it *fair* to ask...? Is it even *possible*...?

Again, please do not make me into a "political extremist" who stands firmly on one side of all partisan issues. I am not at all *that* person. **ANY** law that is put into place that restricts and reduces the number of guns that can be obtained by mentally unhealthy or convicted felons **IS** a **GOOD** thing (certainly will not hurt!). However, here are the questions that *I* feel need to be answered TODAY, and especially after this tragic event has taken place in Uvalde, Texas:

- Are **ALL** schools in our nation equipped to have **ALL** exits locked with a "buzzer system" at the front entrance for visitors to be allowed entry (or not), depending on the purpose they give for visiting? **NO!**
- Are ALL schools in our nation equipped with a security "officer," whether they are current/retired law enforcement or not? **NO!** Mathematically speaking, is it even *possible* to have a trained law enforcement **officer** (current OR retired) in **EVERY** school in our nation? **NO!! There aren't enough out there to even remotely make this happen!**
- Are there enough mental health institutions in our nation to equip the growing number of mental health cases in just our school-aged children? **NO!**
- Are there mental health patients in institutions across our nation who are discharged only because of insurance coverage and not because they are "well" enough to be discharged? **YES!**
- Are there administrations in schools across our nation who have worked hard to **REMOVE** dangerous juveniles from schools (with plenty of documentation and evidence!) only to be forced by the court systems to re-enroll the dangerous juveniles BACK into school to receive their education? **YES!**
- For the vast majority of school shootings that have been documented in our nation up to this very day, aren't nearly ALL of them committed by the hands of current or recent students twenty years old or younger? **YES!**

I hope these questions illustrate my point. **UNTIL** these questions get resolved, there is very little that gun control will do to help diminish or eradicate these violent acts. **THESE** are the questions and topics that I feel need to be addressed by the government and every school district across our nation… and **SOON!**

In the meantime, I can remember saying a good number of prayers over the course of my career as a principal with more frequency at the times that near-violent acts occurred at the school I was responsible for, and especially at the moments that events like Sandy Hook Elementary, Marshall County High School, and Marjory Stoneman Douglas High School took place. I can remember being unable to sleep on many nights as a principal with concerns over the increase in school violence across our nation or the near-violent acts that may have taken place at "my" school. I said a prayer as I was traveling home after graduation last Friday night that I almost included in this journal, but I decided it may not be appropriate. Here is a slightly modified version of this prayer to suit the victims of the Robb Elementary shooting and their families… appropriate or not:

A Retiring HS Principal's Prayer

Thank you, Lord,
for giving me the experiences
I have had over my career.
The connections I have made
with students and the
tremendous adults I have called my peers
have been a blessing to me!

Thank you, Lord,

for keeping the students and staff

safe and protected against harm

as a result of school violence.

I am blessed to have no casualties

at the hands of guns or other weapons

during my time as principal.

Lord, I pray for the victims and families

*of **all** school shootings,*

but especially the victims and families

of the Robb Elementary shooting yesterday.

May the families find peace

after they mourn the loss of their loved ones.

May the leaders of this nation

and the leaders of schools across this nation

find the solutions to prevent

these tragic losses of life in the future. Amen.

May 31, 2022 (Parting Thoughts of a Retiring Educator…) - Although my last day is actually Friday, June 17, today was my last day to occupy the Principal's Office at Apollo HS. I had decided that it makes more sense for my replacement to move in and set his office up than for me to continue coming back to this office, even though I have a few more days left. At this point, all I am needed for is to sign the remaining expenditure paperwork and checks that are necessary to close out the "books" for the year. I get that there is little else for me to do, but it sure seems like a waste of precious time for me to occupy space here at the school between now and June 17. There are other ways I could have handled this, I guess, but this is how I will be finishing my thirty-two year career....

Reflecting back over my time as an educator, it is surreal to consider the number of students whom I have impacted (positive OR negatively!) as a classroom teacher and the number of adults I have worked alongside during that time! I am truly **BLESSED** for all the opportunities that have been presented to me and for the connections that I have been afforded. I firmly believe that "everything happens for a reason" and that the path that I have traveled from the humble beginning of my career until now and the people I have met and worked with along the way have all been a part of **His Plan**. I am so thankful and intend to continue to relay this sentiment for the rest of my years! I can only pray that the time I have remaining on this earth is just as fruitful and rewarding....

Then again, I cannot finish this journal entry without leaving my final thoughts about the concerns that I have highlighted several times in this book and especially Book 1, *Humanity in Peril*. I will summarize the biggest issues that education is dealing with that must be addressed at some point, if there is to be any hope for society, humanity, and our nation moving forward:

- Too many of our nation's school-aged children are **not being raised by their parents**. Some communities show this statistic far more than others, but many of the following concerns stem from issues related to this fact.
- Absenteeism, mental issues, "extreme" behaviors, and apathy

towards education have dramatically increased over the past 5 years. The pandemic is not the culprit that started it all but is definitely responsible for magnifying these concerns.
- Social media platforms are the spawning ground for negativity and hate. There are far more adult **AND** child **BULLIES** today than there have ever been in the history of our country. Too many lives have been lost as a direct result of this statement. Too many lives have been changed forever. Too much property damage has been sustained just in this past year *alone* in schools as a direct reaction for students to "accept a challenge" that has been posted on social media.
  » Too many ADULTS are making all their decisions based on what they see and read on social media.
  » SOME of our parents are the worst role models for school-aged children when it comes to interactions and "bashing" on social media. SOME of our rich and famous individuals in America, as well as elected officials have been horrible role models as well! It is *so irresponsible* to think of the appalling things that have been put into words and shared for *any* eyes in the world to see.
- Where has the respect for education and educators, in general, gone?! This may be one of the more disappointing things that has happened over my thirty-two year career. When I first started in 1990, most households and communities STILL followed the "if you get in trouble in school, you will get it double when you get home" philosophy! Today, more parents or guardians are quick to question their child's teacher (or school), quick to make excuses for their child, or quick to cover up the trouble that took place to warrant discipline. Enough said...! If I go any further on this topic, I may have another book to publish....
- School violence has increased as a result of what has taken place in society over the past decade or more, but the catalyst that started the individuals directing the violence towards

individuals or schools likely originated as a direct result of one or more of the bulleted topics above.
- Last MAJOR concern for education today? There are simply not enough certified teachers in the pipeline to sustain education moving forward! All of the above may be many of the reasons for this fact, but the lack of respect shown by some elected officials for public education and the lack of pay increases over the past decade or more to cover the cost-of-living increases are likely the biggest contributing factors (at least speaking for Kentucky).
  - » As I have mentioned before, FREE PUBLIC EDUCATION FOR ALL **_should be_** something that knows no partisanship.
  - » Our CHILDREN and especially the schools and teachers who educate them **_should be_** a worthy investment!
  - » Citizens who are **_still convinced_** that teachers get paid what they are worth due mostly to the belief that they have summers "off" and they leave every day at 3:00 pm to go home during the school year are living in a fantasy world! Anyone who is married to or closely related to an educator **_knows_** that teachers spend their evenings and parts of their weekend over the course of the school year planning, grading papers, and taking time away from their families! I will fully admit that **_not all teachers_** follow this work regimen throughout the school year, but I would be willing to say that eighty-percent or more I have worked with have! Case in point: I have known too many teachers just since I have been at Apollo HS tell me that they "hate" Sunday afternoons and evenings because of the work they have to prepare for the school week! For all of the items bulleted above, teacher's jobs have become far more difficult (and HAZARDOUS!) than they were thirty-two years ago! Once again, "enough said!"... Teachers need (DESERVE) more pay...!

On the other hand, there **ARE** still some "Glimmers of Hope" that education will survive the test of these hard times that I have tried my best to spotlight in this book. Here are a few that I can say that I am proud to have been a part of:

- My daughter, Lauren, the "glimmer" whom this book was dedicated to, and all pre-educators like her, who are answering the call to be teachers (despite the conditions that may exist today), give us hope for the future of education....
- There are several "Rock Star" teachers who have been highlighted in both books who answered the call to be teachers and will continue answering the call regardless of conditions because it is their true passion! They would not be able to function in the workplace or be happy if they tried to pursue anything else. Whether they go many years beyond the minimum before retiring is an unknown factor for now (depending on their degree of "rock stardom"). **THESE** teachers are the ones that will be most willing to go the distance....
- Conditions in education are (slowly) getting better from the state we were in this past fall semester 2021 when we first came back from the previous "pandemic year." Certainly a lot of work is still needed, but based on the behaviors that reduced over this year at Apollo and the fact that the teaching/learning this year was superior to what took place the previous year under mostly virtual conditions, there is **HOPE** that the academic state of our students will continue to improve... that is... PROVIDED that we can continue these next few years with *uninterrupted in-person learning*!
- A handful of districts in our region in Western-Kentucky, like Daviess Co. Public Schools, have made the decision to increase pay for ALL staff by as much as four-percent. This **IS** good and **LONG** overdue, but it is just the beginning! For the pay to reach a point that it really should be, these three and four-percent raises need to be sustained for the next few years. Districts

alone cannot afford to do this! **Legislators must provide the help to continue budgeting adequately for education to positively move forward.** If this were to occur, THEN we can say that the respect **FOR** teachers (by our lawmakers, at least) has returned. ALSO, when the pay for custodians and cafeteria workers reaches a respectable level, it will be known based on ALL positions filled in schools and no principals being needed to serve as cashier at lunchtime....

Final word regarding the journey that this "last year journal" has been for me... I have to laugh to myself as I am typing these words, thinking back to my thoughts of writing my first journal entry on August 11, 2021. I had no idea that my words would lead to publication of not one, but **TWO** books within the next year! Yes, a story unfolded as I continued writing journal entries in the fall of 2021, and it wasn't until the first week in January 2022 (after consultation from others) that I made the decision to go through with publication....

My only hope is that there are many others who find these words helpful and NOT for the reasons you are thinking. My final reasons for deciding to publish Book 1 had nothing to do with monetary gain. If these publications ARE successful, I will likely donate more than I should BACK in the form of pre-education scholarships at the schools I have worked over my career. **Bottom Line - I want to continue helping educators and education long after my retirement.** If the writing of these books provides the means for me to accomplish this goal, I can consider my purpose and my passion in life fulfilled....

AFTERWORD

Glimmer of Hope...(?)

YES, this "can" has been kicked long enough...! I hope that you have enjoyed the opportunity to read this book as well as Book 1, *Humanity in Peril*. Whether you did or did not, I am hoping that this last bit of advice will prove to be helpful in "sounding the alarm" in an effort to save education. The **_future of humanity_** desperately needs for the following to happen **_as soon as possible_**:

PARENTS of school-aged children -

- LOVE your schools!! Please understand what is at stake. **YOUR CHILD'S success and especially their ability to pursue paths that connect closest to what society needs is dependent upon their K-12 experience**. EVERYONE works at peak performance when they are HAPPY and feel VALUED. Parents who have sent plates of homemade holiday treats to your schools, PLEASE send more! Small gestures like this are so much appreciated...! However, in this day and time, unfortunately the negative comments and interactions that educators are exposed to come most likely at a rate of 50 to 1. Do you want the "Rock Star" teachers to stay in teaching beyond twenty-seven years? Make sure they are HAPPY. ***<u>Parents need to be flooding their schools with gestures of appreciation and constant positivity... You will absolutely notice a difference AND you will LOVE the results...</u>***!

- Those who cannot break away from social media, at least disengage completely with anything related to negative trashing of others. Even better, negativity in general. Social media will continue to be the "downfall of society," in my humble opinion. I, still to this day, REFUSE to even go to that "adult playground" where individuals are bullied repeatedly... DAILY....

- Raise your children to respect those who are responsible for their education AND understand the level that your children are most capable of reaching lies within the hands of their teachers! The more that students vandalize, bully, disrupt the learning process, get into fights, lie, cheat, steal, etc...., the LEAST likely schools and educators will give them a chance. This is good ol' common sense. DISRESPECT at any level does NOT make educators who desire to make a difference want to continue trying.

- VOLUNTEER for your schools - especially in HIGH SCHOOL. Parents in many high schools across the nation are non-existent. If you volunteer one hour per week, it will be eye-opening for you, and I can assure you that it will be VALUED and appreciated by the school.

- Keep in mind that teachers are not any more perfect than any other individual and can make mistakes or poor choices. When mistakes have been made or something needs to be addressed, be prepared to communicate directly to the teacher in a rational and non-combative approach FIRST. Far too many parents are electing to take what they hear from their children and go straight to the principal, or even worse, making first contact with the Board Office. Give each teacher the benefit of the doubt and treat them as professionals, FIRST. If, after having that conversation, you feel that the concerns were not addressed appropriately, it is acceptable to consult with a guidance counselor OR an administrator (depending on the nature of the concern). This is how the process works. I have found when personal conversations take place (especially when parents and teachers have met *in person*) and a rational conversation is involved, the concerns are taken care of OR a much clearer understanding for what is going on occurs, resulting in teacher/parenting "partnerships" in developing a plan for success. It does no good to start conversations by accusing the teacher of doing something they may not have done and especially in a combative "assault." If you follow the "teacher conversation FIRST" protocol that I have described, you have at least given them the professional courtesy of taking care of the issue themselves. This act should weigh heavily in your favor moving forward....

COMMUNITIES -

- RALLY in support of your schools and education in general. Think about what is at stake. How well do you want the children to be educated before being released to society? Do you want certified TEACHERS to educate the children in your community? YES..., of course! Communities had better find ways to support getting the pipeline of teachers filled again and CONTINUE to support educators so that they will teach beyond twenty-seven years.
- Find ways to increase your school's capacity to serve students with mental health needs. This is critical! For rural schools

who may not be near enough to receive resources provided by Regional Mental Health Hospitals, communities must secure methods of providing adequate help for students who need mental health support. Just consider what happens when you don't...!
- ENSURE that your court systems are REMOVING dangerous individuals who continuously disrupt the educational process, break laws, and become threats to the safety of the rest of the student population (and adults!). Chances are YOUR court systems are FORCING schools to take these students back.
- MAKE YOUR SCHOOLS AND TEACHERS FEEL VALUED AND RESPECTED - HAPPY teachers are most likely on their 'A' game....

SCHOOL DISTRICTS -

- I already know you have done everything you can think of to RETAIN your best teachers, SECURE the best candidates for new positions, AND keep your people happy. What is the definition of insanity? Doing the same thing over and over again, expecting different results. Please consider changing your approach (bravo for any school district already working in this direction!):
    » RALLY to find out who the immediate "friends of education" are, and garner their unconditional support. Local newspapers need to INCREASE stories on all the good things that are going on in schools. Local businesses need to INCREASE their publications and marketing showing their LOVE and SUPPORT of their local schools. Churches need to pray for and otherwise support the efforts of educators WEEKLY, or at least monthly.
    » RALLY with other districts in your region to put together

a highly respected team of administrators (and a rock star teacher or two!) to meet with legislators. Better yet, ask to be allowed to join the House Committee of Education after you have gathered all the evidence you need to show the number of empty teaching positions, behavior rate increases in your schools, absenteeism of teachers, absenteeism of students, increase in mental health alerts/cases in schools, and anything else you can use that would explain why teachers are LEAVING their jobs. Remind them what is at stake if teachers are NOT the ones teaching the future of humanity. While you are there and have their attention, REMIND the legislatures that teachers did NOT go into this noble profession to be treated like a robot who could be programmed to teach topics the way parents/government want them to be taught. NOBODY would be an educator if it required being a "puppet" or a "robot" to serve the public's needs....

» <u>DO NOT support walk-outs of any kind</u>. This advice/recommendation will not be popular among some of our teaching unions, but there is a very important question to consider. Can education survive many more events that leave a lasting negative image in the eyes of our public? Walk-outs will **<u>wreck</u>** many of the opportunities of SUPPORT from communities that I have spelled out above. Education's BEST approach at getting the attention it needs **_should be_** strategic and data-driven.

» EVERY district needs to "grow their own" and find an educator who has the coursework needed to teach Introduction to Education dual-credit courses for high school students to take. In the hands of a "Rock Star" teacher, you have the best chance of getting some of your very own students who care for others and want to help shape the future of humanity and consider teaching.

TEACHERS -

- KEEP YOUR HEAD UP!! You **_KNOW_** that schools and society cannot function without you. Rally together in support of each other and help find ways to work through the most critical barriers that prevent you from teaching and your students from learning. This may be different from school to school, community to community. Follow the lead of the "Rock Stars" in your buildings and work to improve each situation created by the barriers that exist.
- Remember that divided as an "Educator Community," you WILL fall! Educators cannot allow things like vaccination status and beliefs, in general, to come between them. Educators NEED to be the MODEL for accepting differences and still having the ability to work together and "shake hands." RESPECTING others for the opinion they have is a trait lost long ago....
- ACCEPT your roles that come with teaching! For the fifteen-percent of the teacher population that this applies to-
  - » You must accept the fact that chaperoning a dance once per year, sponsoring clubs, parent-teacher conferences, AND graduation ceremonies come as a **_part of the job_**. Avoid being the one among your faculty who always finds an excuse to miss these events.
  - » You must accept the fact that GRADING and keeping your gradebook CURRENT is a **_part of the job_**.
  - » Regardless of any help, increases in pay or other benefits that may be on the way, you must accept the responsibility of teaching AND expect that you will be held accountable without question... Just like fifteen-percent of ANY profession, this is what makes **_all educators look bad_** in the eyes of the community...!
- DO NOT accept the invitation to protest publicly or "walkout." Please consider a more strategic plan to get the attention you need (see District, above).

LEGISLATORS -

- Where do I begin…? YOU have the power to make change, provide adequate funding for education, and SEE to it that the pipeline supplying suitable pre-educators is filled once again. YOU have turned your back on educators for far too long! Let us think about what is at stake to continue ignoring this infrastructure agenda item. Are YOU willing to accept the responsibility for non-educators teaching America's children in the very near future?
- Our nation is as DIVIDED now as it has ever been in the darkest history of our country. How has this happened? Quite simply, we are at "war" with each other. This is disappointing, especially considering that our forefathers established this country in the belief that a two-party system should work together and respect the differences that exist… There are certain items that establish a very critical foundation for the continuation of "life, liberty and the pursuit of happiness" for the best interests of GENERATIONS of Americans to come; **_EDUCATION as well as the HEALTH of ALL its citizens MUST be HIGH PRIORITY items_**! It is unacceptable that the conditions in education have reached this point!!
- **_Represent the PEOPLE_** when making decisions and not your own agenda or interest of your party. In Kentucky this past spring 2022, legislators voted FOR House Bill 9 when there was a "tidal wave" of opposition shared by educators by means of phone calls and signed petitions because of the **_reduced funding_** for public education the bill would create. Kentucky's Governor VETOED this bill in April 2022. Legislators tried their best to override this veto to put the contents of HB9 into effect. THANKFULLY, the end result was putting HB9 contents on "pause," but a true democratic functioning government shouldn't have taken the extent of these efforts to pass something that wasn't in education's best interest to begin with….

- When in doubt, refer to my first bullet point advice - ***FUND EDUCATION, FUND EDUCATION, FUND EDUCATION…!***

Legislators, parents, community members, listen up!! Education **NEEDS** your help and deserves your ***RESPECT/SUPPORT***! Please help answer the call…!